First World War
and Army of Occupation
War Diary
France, Belgium and Germany

36 DIVISION
Divisional Troops
Royal Army Medical Corps
110 Field Ambulance
4 October 1915 - 17 June 1919

WO95/2500/1

The Naval & Military Press Ltd
www.nmarchive.com
Published in association with The National Archives

Published by

The Naval & Military Press Ltd

Unit 10 Ridgewood Industrial Park,

Uckfield, East Sussex,

TN22 5QE England

Tel: +44 (0) 1825 749494

www.naval-military-press.com

www.nmarchive.com

This diary has been reprinted in facsimile from the original. Any imperfections are inevitably reproduced and the quality may fall short of modern type and cartographic standards.

© Crown Copyright
Images reproduced by permission of The National Archives, London, England, 2015.

Contents

Document type	Place/Title	Date From	Date To
Heading	WO95/2500/1 110 Field Ambulance		
Heading	36th Division 110th Fld Ambulance 1915 Oct 1919 June		
Heading	36th Division 110th F. Ambulance Vol I Oct 15 121/7592		
Heading	War Diary of 6/8 110 Field Ambulance 4/10/15 To 31/10/15 Vol 1		
War Diary	Bordon	04/10/1915	04/10/1915
War Diary	Havre	05/10/1915	06/10/1915
War Diary	Longueau	07/10/1915	07/10/1915
War Diary	Vignacourt	07/10/1915	22/10/1915
War Diary	Berteaucourt.	22/10/1915	31/10/1915
Heading	36th Division 110th VOL 7a. Vol 2 121/7693 Vol 15		
War Diary	Berteaucourt.	01/11/1915	04/11/1915
War Diary	Puchvillers	05/11/1915	05/11/1915
War Diary	Clairfaye	05/11/1915	30/11/1915
Heading	10th F.A. Vol 3 121/7935. Dec 1915		
War Diary	Clairfaye	01/12/1915	31/12/1915
Heading	War Diary 110th Field Ambulance R.A.M.C. From 1st January 1916 To 31st January 1916		
War Diary	Clairfaye	01/01/1916	31/01/1916
Heading	4th Div to the 4th Feb 1916 34th Div From 4th Feb 1916 To 110 Field Ambulance Feb 1916		
Heading	War Diary 110th Field Ambulance RAMC From Feb 1 To Feb 29th 1916 110. F.A. 36th Div Vol 5		
War Diary	Clairfaye	01/02/1916	29/02/1916
Heading	36th Div A.F.G. 2118 War Diary 110th Field Ambulance R.A.M.C. B.E.F. from 1st March 1916 to 31st March 1916 Vol 6 1 1107 Amb Vol 6		
War Diary	Clairfaye	01/03/1916	31/03/1916
Heading	War Diary of 110th Field Ambulance R.A.M.C. From April 1st 1916 To April 31st 1916 Volume 7 36th Div		
War Diary	Clairfaye	01/04/1916	30/04/1916
Heading	War Diary 110th Field Ambulance From May 1st 1916 To May 31st 1916 Volume VIII		
War Diary	Clairfaye	28/04/1916	31/05/1916
Heading	War Diary of 110th Field Ambulance From 1st June. 1916 To 30 June 1916 Volume IX Vol 9 June		
War Diary	Clairfaye	01/06/1916	30/06/1916
Heading	War Diary Of 110th Field Ambulance R.A.M.C. From 1st July 1916 To July 31st 1916 Volume X A.f.C 2118 36 July 110 F.A.M.G.		
War Diary	Clairfaye	01/07/1916	05/07/1916
War Diary	Septenville	05/07/1916	10/07/1916
War Diary	Behuval	11/07/1916	11/07/1916
War Diary	Prouville	11/07/1916	12/07/1916
War Diary	Conteville	12/07/1916	12/07/1916
War Diary	Berguette	12/07/1916	12/07/1916
War Diary	Campagne	13/07/1916	13/07/1916
War Diary	Westrove	13/07/1916	20/07/1916

War Diary	Volkerinckhove	21/07/1916	21/07/1916
War Diary	Wormhoute	21/07/1916	22/07/1916
War Diary	Le Brearde	22/07/1916	23/07/1916
War Diary	Bailleul	23/07/1916	31/07/1916
Heading	B.E.F. Summary Of Medical War Diaries Of 110th F.A. 36th Div. 8th Corps. 5th Army. 19th Corps From 26th July. 4th Corps 3rd Army From 23rd August.		
Miscellaneous	110th F.A. 36th Div. 8th Corps. 5th Army. Officer Commanding-Lt. Col. B.H.V. Dunbar. 19th Corps From 26th July.	26/07/1916	26/07/1916
Miscellaneous	110th F.A. 36th Div. 19th Corps. 5th Army. Officer Commanding-Lt. Col. B.H.V. Dunbar. Major R.G. herewith to o.c. from 15th August.	15/08/1916	15/08/1916
Miscellaneous	110th F.A. 36th Div. Corps. 5th Army. Officer Commanding-Lt. Col. R.H.V. Dunbar. 19th Corps From 26th July.	26/07/1916	26/07/1916
Miscellaneous	110th F.A. 36th Div. 19th Corps. 5th Army. Officer Commanding-Lt. Col B.H.V. Dunbar. Major R.G. Meredith to O.C. From 15th August.	15/08/1916	15/08/1916
Heading	War Diary Of 110th Field Ambulance R.A.M.C. From August 1st 1916 To August 31st 1916 Volume XI August 31st 1916 36th (Wester) Div		
War Diary	Bailleul	01/08/1916	31/08/1916
War Diary	36th Div War Diary 110th Field Ambulance From Sept 1st 1916 To Sept 30th 1916 Volume XII		
War Diary	Bailleul	01/09/1916	30/09/1916
Heading	36th Div. 110th Field Ambulance Oct 1916		
War Diary	Bailleul	01/10/1916	31/10/1916
Heading	36th Div 110th Field Ambulance. Nov 1916 140/1262		
War Diary	Bailleul	01/11/1916	30/11/1916
Heading	36th Div 110th Field Ambulance Dec 1916 140/1962		
War Diary	Bailleul	01/12/1916	31/12/1916
Heading	36th Div 110th Field Ambulance 140/1943 36 Jan 1917		
War Diary	Bailleul	01/01/1917	31/01/1917
Heading	36th Div. 110th Field Ambulance. 140/1917 Feb 1917		
War Diary	Bailleul	01/02/1917	28/02/1917
Heading	36th Div 110th Field Ambulance Mar. 1917 140/2042		
War Diary	Bailleul	01/03/1917	31/03/1917
Heading	110th F.A. 140/2086 April 1917		
War Diary	Bailleul	01/04/1917	30/04/1917
Heading	No.110 F.A. May. 1917 140/2161		
War Diary	Bailleul	01/05/1917	31/05/1917
Heading	No. 110 F.A. 140/2230 June 1917 5		
War Diary	Bailleul	01/06/1917	06/06/1917
War Diary	N 31.c.3.5.	07/06/1917	08/06/1917
War Diary	Lindenhoek	08/06/1917	10/06/1917
War Diary	Bailleul	11/06/1917	19/06/1917
War Diary	Locre	19/06/1917	29/06/1917
War Diary	Meteran	29/06/1917	30/06/1917
Heading	July 1917 S No. 110 F.A. 140/2298		
War Diary	Meteren	01/07/1917	05/07/1917
War Diary	Caestre	05/07/1916	06/07/1916
War Diary	Renescure	07/07/1917	07/07/1917
War Diary	La Wattine	07/07/1917	20/07/1917
War Diary	Esquerdes	20/07/1917	25/07/1917
War Diary	Setques	25/07/1917	25/07/1917

War Diary	Wennizeele	25/07/1917	25/07/1917
War Diary	Ouder Eele	26/07/1917	30/07/1917
War Diary	Watau	31/07/1917	31/07/1917
War Diary	Watau K14.c.9.8.	31/07/1917	31/07/1917
Heading	No. 110. 7.C. Aug 1917 S 140/2304		
Miscellaneous	Summary Of Medical War Diaries Of 110th F.A. 36th Div. 8th Corps. 5th Army. 19th Corps From 26th July. 4th Corps 3rd Army From 23rd August.	23/08/1917	23/08/1917
Miscellaneous			
Miscellaneous	110th F.A. 36th Div. 19th Corps. 5th Army. Officer Commanding-Major R.G. Meredith. 4th Corps. 3rd Army From 23rd August.	23/08/1917	23/08/1917
Miscellaneous			
Miscellaneous	110th F.A. 36th Div. 19th Corps. 5th Army. Officer Commanding-Major R.G. Meredith. 4th Corps, 3rd Army From 23rd August.	23/08/1917	23/08/1917
War Diary	Watau K 24 C. 9.8.	01/08/1917	06/08/1917
War Diary	Hilhoek	07/08/1917	15/08/1917
War Diary	Poperinghe. G 11.a.4.6.	15/08/1917	15/08/1917
War Diary	G11.a.4.6.	16/08/1917	17/08/1917
War Diary	Winizeele. J17a34.	18/08/1917	20/08/1917
War Diary	Lechelle P 31 a 5.9.	24/08/1917	25/08/1917
War Diary	Bus. O 23.d.6.4.	28/05/1917	30/05/1917
Heading	No. 110 F.A. Sept. 1917 140/2438		
War Diary	Bus. O 23.d.6.2. Sheet 57.c.	04/09/1917	30/09/1917
Heading	No. 110 F.A. Oct. 1917 140/2699		
Heading	No. 110. F.A. Nov. 1917		
War Diary	Bus O23d.6.2. Sheet 57.c.	01/11/1917	16/11/1917
War Diary	Lebuquiere	17/11/1917	18/11/1917
War Diary	J 29	19/11/1917	20/11/1917
War Diary	J29.a.5.6.	21/11/1917	27/11/1917
War Diary	Bernaville.	26/11/1917	30/11/1917
War Diary	Courlelle Le. Comte.	30/11/1917	30/11/1917
Heading	No.110. F.A. 140/2618		
War Diary	Beaulencourt	01/12/1917	01/12/1917
War Diary	Lechelle	02/12/1917	02/12/1917
War Diary	Moislans.	04/12/1917	08/12/1917
War Diary	Etricourt.	15/12/1917	15/12/1917
War Diary	Lucheux	16/12/1917	16/12/1917
War Diary	Beaudricourt.	17/12/1917	24/12/1917
War Diary	Corbie (Le Nenviul).	27/12/1917	27/12/1917
Heading	No. 110. F.A. 140/2696. Jan 1918		
War Diary	Corbie.	04/01/1918	04/01/1918
War Diary	Rosiers.	07/01/1918	07/01/1918
War Diary	Bethencourt	09/01/1918	09/01/1918
War Diary	Dury.	11/01/1918	31/01/1918
Heading	War Diary Of 110th Field Ambulance. From 1st February 1918 To 28th February 1918. Vol. XXIX.		
War Diary	Dury	01/02/1918	28/02/1918
Heading	War Diary Of 110th Field Ambulance. From 1st March 1918 To 31st March 1918. Vol. XXX		
War Diary	Annois	01/03/1918	21/03/1918
War Diary	St. Simon	21/03/1918	21/03/1918
War Diary	Annois	21/03/1918	21/03/1918
War Diary	Brouchy	22/03/1918	23/03/1918
War Diary	Berlancourt	23/03/1918	24/03/1918

War Diary	Amy.	24/03/1918	24/03/1918
War Diary	Warsy	25/03/1918	26/03/1918
War Diary	Grivesnes	26/03/1918	27/03/1918
War Diary	Aubvillers.	27/03/1918	27/03/1918
War Diary	Chirmont.	27/03/1918	28/03/1918
War Diary	Lawarde	28/03/1918	28/03/1918
War Diary	La. Faloise	28/03/1918	29/03/1918
War Diary	Wailly	29/03/1918	29/03/1918
War Diary	I Mile From Nampauval	30/03/1918	30/03/1918
War Diary	Saleux.	31/03/1918	31/03/1918
War Diary	Courtieux	31/03/1918	31/03/1918
Heading	War Diary Of 110th Field Ambulance From 1st April 1918 To 30th April 1918 Volume XXXI 140/2900		
War Diary	Courtieux.	01/04/1918	04/04/1918
War Diary	Fouquieres.	04/04/1918	04/04/1918
War Diary	Proven.	05/04/1918	05/04/1918
War Diary	Nospitalfarm Camp.	05/04/1918	05/04/1918
War Diary	L'Ebbe Farm.	06/04/1918	27/04/1918
War Diary	Tubby. Camp.	27/04/1918	30/04/1918
Heading	War Diary of 110th Field Ambulance May 1918 Volume XXXII 140/2983		
War Diary	Tubby Camp. W.17.d.5.7. Sheet 19 Belgium & France	01/05/1918	07/05/1918
War Diary	Tubby Camp. W.17.d.6.7.	08/05/1918	16/05/1918
War Diary	Tubby Camp Sheet 19. (W.27.d.6.7.)	17/05/1918	26/05/1918
War Diary	Tubby Camp	28/05/1918	31/05/1918
Heading	June 1918, 110th F.A. 140/3131.		
War Diary	Tubby Camp. W. 17.d.6.7. Sheet.19. Belgium & France	01/06/1918	30/06/1918
Miscellaneous	Medical Arrangements 2 Hour. (Major Operations) Appendix No 1	18/07/1918	18/07/1918
War Diary	Tubby Camp. W. 17.d.6.7. Sheet 19. B. & France	01/06/1918	06/06/1918
War Diary	O.24.d.5.9.	07/06/1918	07/06/1918
War Diary	Q.22.C.31.	07/06/1918	30/06/1918
Miscellaneous	Medical Arrangements. 110th Field Ambulance. Appendix No 1		
Heading	Aug. 1918 110th F.A. 140/3200		
War Diary	Q.22.c.1.3.	01/08/1918	29/08/1918
War Diary	G. 15.A.5.9. Sheet 27. 13a.F.	30/08/1918	30/08/1918
War Diary	G.15.a.5.9.	31/08/1918	31/08/1918
War Diary	H.29.d.4.8.	31/08/1918	31/08/1918
War Diary	Ochtezeele H.29.d.4.8.	01/09/1918	24/09/1918
War Diary	St. Jan De Biezen	27/09/1918	28/09/1918
War Diary	Ypres	29/09/1918	29/09/1918
Heading	Oct 1918 110th F.A.		
War Diary	School House Ypres	01/10/1918	06/10/1918
War Diary	Infantry Bles. Ypres.	07/10/1918	12/10/1918
War Diary	Becelaere	14/10/1918	14/10/1918
War Diary	Dadizeele	15/10/1918	17/10/1918
War Diary	Ledeghem	19/10/1918	19/10/1918
War Diary	Lendelede.	20/10/1918	25/10/1918
War Diary	Deerlyck	26/10/1918	27/10/1918
War Diary	Aelbeke	28/10/1918	29/10/1918
Heading	Nov. 1918. 110th F.A. 140/3401		
War Diary	Aelbeke	02/11/1918	03/11/1918
War Diary	Mouscron	04/11/1918	30/11/1918
Heading	Dec 1918 No. 110 F.A.		
War Diary	Mouskeron.	01/12/1918	31/12/1918

Heading	No. 110 F.A. June 1919 140/2496		
War Diary	Mouscron.	01/01/1919	18/01/1919
War Diary	Mohskeron	19/01/1919	31/01/1919
War Diary	No 110 Field Ambulance 146/3529 Feb 1919		
War Diary	Mouskeron	01/02/1919	28/02/1919
Heading	Mar. 1919 No. F.A. 140/3551		
War Diary	Mar 1919	01/03/1919	30/03/1919
Heading	Apr 19		
War Diary	Monsoon	03/04/1919	28/04/1919
Heading	May 1919		
War Diary	Monsoon	08/05/1919	18/05/1919
Heading	June 110th F.A. 140/3585		
War Diary		06/06/1919	17/06/1919

WO/95/2500/11

110 Field Ambulance.

36TH DIVISION

110TH FLD AMBULANCE

1915 OCT ~~FEB 1916-DEC 1918~~ 1919 JUNE

14/7597

36th K. wown

110th F. Ambulance
Vol I
Oct 15

Oct-1915

Confidential
War Diary
of
HQ 110th Fd Ambulance

3/10/15

4/10/15

Col 1

WAR DIARY
or
INTELLIGENCE SUMMARY.
(Erase heading not required.)

Army Form C. 2118.

Place	Date	Hour	Summary of Events and Information	Remarks and references to Appendices
BORDON	4/10/15	4.50 am	First party left camp at OXNEY FARM to entrain for SOUTHAMPTON	
		5.50 am	Second party left camp at OXNEY FARM to entrain for SOUTHAMPTON.	
			Entraining carried out without a hitch in fine time.	
		6.5 am	First party arrived at SOUTHAMPTON and detrained	
		7.5 am	Second party arrived at SOUTHAMPTON and detrained. Horses, mules and men marched to the docks by the Veterinary Officer and arrangements obtained. Men remained in a shed on the docks all day till it was time to embark.	
		3.30 pm	Embarked on S.S. AUSTRALIND (Capt ANGEL). Men were accommodated in the tween decks and horses on the 2nd Deck. O.C. Troops Capt PEARSON 1/3 LONDON Bde Ammunition Column.	
		5 pm	Sailed from SOUTHAMPTON. Journey uneventful.	
HAVRE	5/10/15	7 am	Arrived & started disembarking forthwith. Disembark completed by 10 am	
		10 am	Received orders for entrainment.	
		11.30 am	Moved off to H.S. Rest Camp	
		12.15 am	Arrived at Rest Camp & reported to the Camp Commandant	

WAR DIARY
or
INTELLIGENCE SUMMARY.
(Erase heading not required.)

Army Form C. 2118.

Place	Date	Hour	Summary of Events and Information	Remarks and references to Appendices
HAVRE	6/5/15	2 pm	Sent Capt. EWING & Lieut. EMERSON to cant. commandant to receive instructions as to route & to arrange for the guard. Party & men ready to the Railway Station for entrainment. Raining all day.	
		2.30 pm	Reveille	
		3.30 am	Ration party under Lieut. EMERSON left for the Station to draw rations.	
		4. am	Remainder of the Force then between left for Station.	
		5.30	Arrived at point 3. of entrainment – Raining all the time.	
		6. am	Started entraining. I am O.C. train – Rations issued.	
		8.19 am	Left HAVRE	
LONGUEAU	"	1.30 pm	Coffee served out to the men	
		5.50 pm	Arrived in place of detrainment – Detrained & received orders to proceed to VIGNACOURT by route march.	AMIENS Sheet 12
VIGNACOURT	7/5/15	7.30 pm	Left LONGUEAU via AMIENS, ST VAAST EN CHAUSSEE	
		1. AM	Arrived – Men marched well. Rout was arduous. Some showed the ends of been brought down absolutely about 16 miles. Have put out, the men by interpreter also	etc.
			accident billets for Officers & men –	

WAR DIARY
or
INTELLIGENCE SUMMARY.

(Erase heading not required.)

Army Form C. 2118.

Instructions regarding War Diaries and Intelligence
Summaries are contained in F. S. Regs., Part II.
and the Staff Manual respectively. Title pages
will be prepared in manuscript.

Place	Date	Hour	Summary of Events and Information	Remarks and references to Appendices
VIGNACOURT	7/15	4 am	Billeting completed. Most of the billets were very bad & very insanitary & the unit was spread over a very large area	AMIENS Sheet 12
VIGNACOURT	7/15	11 am	Found a large barn to accommodate the whole unit except officers. Straw was obtained for the billets. There was some difficulty in getting returns.	
		3 pm	Established a temporary Dressing Station for sick. Accommodation very inadequate. A few minor cases were dealt with.	do
do	8/15	9 am	A few cases admitted to dressing Station. Had a visit from Adams and Dasens who inspected the men's billets	do
		2 pm	Seven motor ambulances and one motor bicycle arrived.	
"	9/15	9 am	Sent one motor ambulance to accompany the 107th Bde to the area occupied by the 4th Div.	do
			The present Dressing Station is very unsuitable and steps are being taken to secure a more suitable building. But it is very difficult as all the houses here are occupied.	
			Sent Lieuts. Gunison & Pearse to report to No. 11 and 12 Field Ambulances for three days training at BERTRANCOURT and FORCEVILLE.	

1577 Wt. W10791/1773 500,000 1/15 D. D. & L.   A.D.S.S./Forms/C. 2118.

WAR DIARY
or
INTELLIGENCE SUMMARY.
(Erase heading not required.)

Army Form C. 2118.

Place	Date	Hour	Summary of Events and Information	Remarks and references to Appendices
VIGNACOURT	10/2/15	6 pm	Motor ambulance sent W.O.II – 109. Bolt nothing this evening	AMIENS Sheet 12
do	11/2/15	10 am	Amiens. Drilling minor. Drawing extra – Sent orderly to arrange a hairdressing for – Drawing station	do
do	12/2/15	9 am	Got a cape interment for a Drawing station – But is in pressure respect by the A.D.M.S. in an evening for one. The place is very dirty	do
"	6 pm		2nd Price, Pension arrived from the 4th Divn.	
"	6 pm		Previous marcher from Amiens to paid myself at BERTRANCOURT for 3 days training.	do
do	13/2/15	6 am	Left VIGNACOURT by own ambulance to report to No 11 F.A.	do
do	16/2/15	6 pm	Returns from the 4th Divn amb – During my absence to D.M.S. X-Corps & Amiens 36 Divn visits the Drawing field and arranged that I obtain	do
			then a Divisional air Fren – & the transport I thank and ordered was repaid there from the Divns.	
do	17/2/15	8 am	Lieut Hay & Corney left for their keep training with the 4th Divn.	do
		2 pm	Amiens Came over to arrange about – Divisive Pers Frais. List Divn's when I are arrangements were made to talk the	

Place	Date	Hour	Summary of Events and Information	Remarks and references to Appendices
VIGNACOURT	18/12	9 am	Matter in hand at once. Captain Davis — Sanitary Officer & Lieut Brown 16/Division arrived & arrange about forming small sets up for Levies, uniforms, stores & get Divisional Cards & this is now. Sick are already arriving from the 10th & 119 Brit Ambulances. Beds the floor in one grade in receiving room yet.	AMIENS Sheet 12
do	19/12	9 am	Men S.O. came & Sanitor in Brig. Dont Present — Very difficult in every installment at present as the means for obtaining hot water is very inadequate.	do
do	20/12	6 am	Lieut Patrick & Capt O'Heit arrived & set above. for transomy — Lieut Hay & Corey returned. Work for improving buildings of Nont Féti Committee.	do
"		6 pm	Received news & arrived not in — this day with the 107 Brigade - C. Sevin under Capt Evans in charge of this.	do
do	21/12	8 am	C. Sevin left to field hay — Received message from Orders & oy that the Division are forming morning next day & to make arrangement for the move —	do
"		12 m	Capt O'Heit & Lieut Patrick returned from the 4th Brit Press in a enrol course of cars & from the 109, 109 — Brit Ambulances.	do

WAR DIARY or INTELLIGENCE SUMMARY

Army Form C. 2118.

Remarks and references to Appendices: **AMIENS** Sheet 12.

Place	Date	Hour	Summary of Events and Information
VIGNACOURT	22/5/15	12 mid.t	Received orders to move from VIGNACOURT to BERTENCOURT. Orders to march in rear of 107 Bde - to be ready to move off in 2 hrs. Issued orders accordingly.
do	"	9. am	Started to load the wagons preparing to move off.
do	"	10. am	Court Martial held on Pte. Farris Murray for drunkenness.
do	"	10.30 am	Evans 65 o/r. reveived & 5 officers. Sent Billeting Officer in advce (Capt O'Neil)
do	"	1.30 pm	Inspected all billets & found all correct.
do	"	2.30 pm	Left VIGNACOURT. Total o/r and 61 cars & trains
BERTENCOURT	"	3.30 pm	Arrived & met by Capt O'Neil who shew in 6 am billets. Found that no billets had been laid off for one of the Bdes. Eventually had 6 hrs in arrival of the personnel & found them with others to work room for each.
do	"	5.30 pm	All men settled in their billets which were no quicker or satisfactory. Rear [?] of the mess in great condition.
do	23/5/15	10. am	Went to an address re Divisive Nest details to say the men can ameliorate accommodation.

WAR DIARY
INTELLIGENCE SUMMARY

(Erase heading not required.)

Army Form C. 2118.

Place	Date	Hour	Summary of Events and Information	Remarks and references to Appendices
BERTRANCOURT	23/12/15	3 pm	Arrived at Arras. Office of intelligence at embarking area. Brought back Major A.B. Burn 15 & took him to our Bn Hd & our to our Train for Divisional Bath.	AMIENS Sheet 12
do	24/12/15	10 am	Arras. Darnet came in to arrange about our Train being ready, & went. Next train went to St. OUEN but could not find any/thing our Train.	do
do	"	1 pm	Went round to the EAST end of the village & found same our train places.	do
do	"	2 pm	Went to Arras to report — he came with me & spoke to the person who he knew our Train.	do
do	"	6.30 pm	Went to the Bde Office to arrange about taking over their bivouacs as they are at present occupied by the 10th Rifles, R.B.& Scotts, who would be moved.	do
do	25/12/15	10 am	Met the Staff Captain & arranged about taking over the bivouacs. Sent 3. Hooded Ambulances to re-accompany the 107th Bde trans. A.D. O'Keefe.	do

WAR DIARY
or
INTELLIGENCE SUMMARY

Army Form C. 2118.

(Erase heading not required.)

Place	Date	Hour	Summary of Events and Information	Remarks and references to Appendices
HEADQRS RE	25/7/15	11.30 am	Sent Cpl. Murray & the A.P.M. to meet up a 2nd party R.O.R. 21 arrested by the S.C.M. AMIENS Station on [previous?] yesterday. He on return to [went?] & [visited?] at establish G.R.P.	Sheet 12
		3 pm	[Orderlies?] & [others?] went to see the proposed building to be used. Rout took [Sen?] Merino mange from Arleux to establish Office [Common?] & Supervise the accommodation of the 15t Bn. [Brit?] Sent him 6 O.R. & [men?] a provision. [ ] en route attending to new Items [re cars?] a provision.	do
do	26/7/15	10 am	Took our new building to the [ ] [Nord?] Station - [Men?] in and started cleaning up - the [Nera?] is very busy, [ ] of our hiders to the 10t A.S.P. Capt. EMERSON went over to the hotel to put in nice working order.	do
		3 pm -	[ ] [arrangement?] of [Staff?] arrived from entrance to new in [ ] [Nord?] Station	
do	27/7/15	10 am	[Seemed?] the Petronage [ ] use of this Ann Luxeuse. [ ] [better?] puting [some?] one [ ] in our.	do
		1.30 pm	Sent out party of 60 OR Serd. Brett.	
		2.30 pm	Sent second party to Serd. Brett.	
		3.30 pm	Sent this party of 60 OR Serd. Brett.	
		9 am	Remainder of units sent to Serd. Brett.	

WAR DIARY
or
INTELLIGENCE SUMMARY.
(Erase heading not required.)

Army Form C. 2118.

Instructions regarding War Diaries and Intelligence Summaries are contained in F. S. Regs., Part II and the Staff Manual respectively. Title pages will be prepared in manuscript.

Place	Date	Hour	Summary of Events and Information	Remarks and references to Appendices
BERTEAUCOURT	28/8/15	3 pm	Paid into Field Ambulance.	AMIENS Sheet 12
	"	5 pm	Message from Adm'g to ask if I was ready to move and if so the Rest Station. Answered Yes I was. Heavy rain all day.	
do	"	9.30 pm	Received orders C Tent parts to Brie this Evening. Orders cancelled.	do
	"	10 pm		
do	29/8/15	11 am	D.M.S. & 2/ Corps (Colonel SWAN) visited the Rest Station this morning.	
	"	2 pm	Elements and care of our patients Extein ? firm.	
do	30/8/15	3.15 pm	Adm'g 3 F.S.O.L. visited the Divisional Rest Station.	
			Received orders to move 113 P.S.O.L. & 110 P.A. have been ordered to hold going outsight viz 12 A.M. & 11.0 P.M.	
				B.M. Juan answered word this answered Noon 11.30 this O.R. 11.0 31/8/15

36 M K Loosan — 4. Nov. 1915
when joined the 4th Div.

110th 7a.
Vol 2

121/7693

Nov. 15

Nov 1915

WAR DIARY or INTELLIGENCE SUMMARY

Army Form C. 2118

Instructions regarding War Diaries and Intelligence Summaries are contained in F. S. Regs., Part II. and the Staff Manual respectively. Title Pages will be prepared in manuscript.

(Erase heading not required.)

Place	Date	Hour	Summary of Events and Information	Remarks and references to Appendices
BERTEAU COURT	1/1/15	10 a.m.	Sgt. Bruey - days visit "Jogging" remanded for trial by Court Martial.	AM12ENS SHUTTER
		3 pm	Detailed address by the G.O.C.	
		9 pm	Received orders for the unit for tomorrow's transports by the D.D. & S.T. Orders received and details in tent orders issued for the parade on the division exercise next day	
do	2/1/15	9 a.m.	Received completed motor ambulance convoy [?] to Divisional Exercise.	
		9.30	Attrive 10: F.A. at CLAIRFAYE. C. Section under Capt. O'NEILL went to Divisional Exercise.	
		10.30	All transports paraded for inspection by the D.D.S.T. next day	
do	3/1/15	9 am	Started to pack up the F.A. equipment for the move.	
		4/1 pm	The ADMS 36th Div. addressed the F.A. before its departure.	
do	4/1/15	10.to 5 am	Left trucks for move to PUCHVILLERS. A.Y.C. section marched via 1 Sept B. Austin behind to head on to the 10th F.A. PUCHVILLERS — TALMAS — PUCHVILLERS. Busies for Marched in NAOURS — TALMAS — PUCHVILLERS. Busies for the night — very bad times — Could not get any train to officers. Emotionary bad to sleep in a school room in the stores.	
PUCHVILLERS	5/1/15	8 am	Left in a car for CLAIRFAYE to start taking over the Brid. Neo. Train the rest of the F.A. left on RAINCHEVAL — ARQUEVES — LEALVILLERS.	
		10 am		

Army Form C. 2118

WAR DIARY
or
INTELLIGENCE SUMMARY
(Erase heading not required.)

Instructions regarding War Diaries and Intelligence Summaries are contained in F. S. Regs., Part II. and the Staff Manual respectively. Title Pages will be prepared in manuscript.

Place	Date	Hour	Summary of Events and Information	Remarks and references to Appendices
CLAIR FAYE	5/7/15	12.30 pm	The F.A. arrived. Proceeded to take on the new Section.	AMIENS See 12
		2 pm	The arrival of the 10th F.A. left. One senior Left behind for the handing over	
	6/7/15	10 am	Received orders to send an Officer to O.P. 12 F.A. Sent Capt O'NEILL	
	7/7/15	10 am	Pte. Cpl. EMERSON in charge of the Officers Mess. Pvt. Freri - G.O.C. 107 Bde. made the round of the Section. One one of S.T.O. reported to a dump & Bde. Office. Very unsatisfactory morning	
		2 pm	arrived at S. Bat. Pvt & Asst. Officer reviewed and Officer interviewing	
	8/7/15	10 am	Half. camp & Supply convoy. Sent drink H.Q. Dud and 3 men – B. men Sept. SKEELY Return lists by F.G.C. Marie for turning. Subsection G to arrive with the Mounting, & 3 men G.T. helped Return G.E. Ashe to supply section in the Office and from to our arrival. Shaved – Rametis from Austhalias and Mess + with + the Plant	
	9/7/15	12 m	Stains Ottawa Brussels Note etc. Chan any and every second Taken	
	10/7/15	11 am	Arrived our companion in entire. Please suing many more & every undertaken from the entered Troop Officers Marci - B. Scorrin	
		2.30pm	Arrived & AMIENS. No field in my wishes extering and 6	
		5pm	Arrived Amiens spent visiting with Field & lute from railway and 6	
		6 pm	Notes from @ AMIENS. Found came G. & 12 R.O. on the place 2 hrg morning 14th and to the team came out visited an influence	
			put wire to keep any out which accepts Service	
	11/7/15	7 pm	Went to Arras and visit G. & 12 R.O. by motor and return G. Pete 3 Hrs + from Town lap Th	
		9.30 am	Went to Arras where his visited for mounting to Arras. Came for Evening on the Station then the Town came on in The	

WAR DIARY
or
INTELLIGENCE SUMMARY

(Erase heading not required.)

Army Form C. 2118

Instructions regarding War Diaries and Intelligence Summaries are contained in F.S. Regs., Part II. and the Staff Manual respectively. Title Pages will be prepared in manuscript.

Place	Date	Hour	Summary of Events and Information	Remarks and references to Appendices
CLAIRFAYE	11/1/15	10 am	Went to RE Yard to get the lorry. Cameras & 3 orderlies took in aviation, and 3 proceeded to	AMIENS Sheet 12.
	"	4.15 pm	Mission taken from Achiet to Bertrancourt	
	"	5 pm	1 mosaic 6 m⁼ 12 RA on FORCEVILLE for instructions & to RFC/planes	
			Ent from H⁼11 and 12 RA & A's taken over in the afternoon. Very late	
12/1/15	9.30 am		Section from H⁼ 12 & A aviation , Bessau on arrival at Aeroplane	"
		10 am	Section from H⁼ 11 RA	
			Section from H⁼12 aviation , C Quentin sector now in the present	
			from 11.1.12 into H⁼6 - 1.1.15 needed & had being but in general	
			on - day into Slaving - Revise 1st sketch for testing -	
13/1/15	9 am		Contact the training of battalion , interpretating the present programmy	"
	"	11 am	visit from Arsenal & Revision interest to Aeroplane of H⁼ 11	
			in to come from aviation. Taking over the 2 cam	
			Print at no BC , H⁼11 to manage about print in the house. Our hour day	
	"	2.30 pm	Ent area from H⁼11 and point in the house. Our hour day	
	"	5 pm	4.0 prints arrived.	
14/1/15	9 am		Continued work & evening brief in	
	"	11.30 am	Visits from Arsenal -	
15/1/15	9 am		Ent. from aviation , satisfactory -	
	"	11.30 am	Visit from Arsenal - the are writer the Officer next Station	"
	"	1 pm	Visit from Dassus - Revise interest of election the Supports -	
	"	4 pm	Ent from H/C & here print for current & circulation in the same Back-	
	"	6.pm		from ACHEUX Sp. J. SKELLY returns to C.n. print -

M1875 Wt. W593/826 1,000,000 4/15 T.B&A. Ad.S&S./Forms/C.2118/14

War Diary or Intelligence Summary

Army Form C. 2118

(Erase heading not required.)

Instructions regarding War Diaries and Intelligence Summaries are contained in F.S. Regs., Part II. and the Staff Manual respectively. Title Pages will be prepared in manuscript.

Place	Date	Hour	Summary of Events and Information	Remarks and references to Appendices
LAIRFAYE	16/1/15	9 a.m.	Heavy fire of enemy. Hard frost at night.	AMIENS Photo
do	17/1/15	10 a.m.	Pte FISHER A.S.C. remanded for hate by Court Martial.	Photo
		11 a.m.	Lt. Col. McALISTER. O.C. 4th Bde Fd inspected the transport & approved.	
			arriving up of W.O.'s farm to use to arm W.O. &	
			Farrier to his company for training - given permission	
	18/1/15	3 p.m.	Went to AMIENS - Visit from ALLARD	—
		5 p.m.	Farrier MURRAY returns from hospital - 20 days F.P. No. 1.	
	19/1/15	9 a.m.	Very cold & frosty morning - Stores taken in stock from 117/12 R.A.S	—
		3 p.m.	Visit from Arens	
		4 p.m.	Pay out	
		6 p.m.	6th A. Session	
			a call of suspects dispatched - attended to DRs on the 12th but send him	6
			on the 16th: Examined & refused C.C.S.;	
			him in the same but have been ordered	
	20/1/15	9 a.m.	Reports case of suspected to ACENS; sent for our doctor who	
			disinfect but.	
		3 p.m.	Visit from Arens. Everything seems in order — disinfection but.	—
	22/1/15	11 a.m.	D.M.S. 3rd Army inspected the dist. Gen. Sloane.	
			Dr FISHER with Lt. G.C.M. Lieut PATRICK promised.	
	23/1/15	3 p.m.	Visit from Arens. Given advantage of cook. Very diffrent	—
			to evening - Drying clothes.	

WAR DIARY or INTELLIGENCE SUMMARY

Army Form C. 2118

Place	Date	Hour	Summary of Events and Information	Remarks and references to Appendices
CLAIRFAYE	24/15	9 am	Received proceedings F.G.C.M. on Dr. Prisoner A.S.C. Sentence to 60 days F.P.N°1	herein shewn
		10 am	Went to see Officer re sudden conversion.	
		2 pm	Promulgation of sentence on Dr. Prisoner by Prison M/Y. Newell. Had an escort	
		11 pm	Stephen McCARTHY – 2/52 Coy R.E. brought in arrest by M/Y Anderson for TOUTENCOURT. He was out of barracks after the hour of curfew could not give any satisfactory reason – Been drinking injured.	
	25/15	2 pm	Went out to the funeral of our native servant – Private Stephen McCARTHY in cemetery at VARENNES – Shot some during the day	
	26/15	9 am	Sent to MARIEUX to 2 new cases selected to the Divisional Gas Station – Had front and nape cases. Come very slowly – very hard to treat	
		2 pm	This morning in the woods.	
	27/15	11 am	Visits from Adlams. Supplies repeated ? came on absentee roms.	
			Visits from Adlams ? D arms. Inspection of breeching & arms. Inspection	
	28/15	9.30 am	Paid out B. Section	
		8 am	Went to an address re [?] & to mob[?] Battle huts. Hard frost	
			Church Parade –	
	30"	2.15	Case of Measles admitted from Dr. Sueste to P.C. 12 – F.A. Continue inoculations, one inoculation to H.C.C.S. Reports to Adms, wires for San Reserve to this unit & lantern	
		10 am	D.M.S. 3rd Army visit Post Stores – extra enemies of blankets	
		12 m		

B.H. Wells Parker
Major ? O.C. 110 F. Amb.

110 R̃ F.A.
Pol: 3

12/7935

Dec 1916

WAR DIARY or INTELLIGENCE SUMMARY

Army Form C. 2118

(Erase heading not required.)

Instructions regarding War Diaries and Intelligence Summaries are contained in F.S. Regs., Part II. and the Staff Manual respectively. Title Pages will be prepared in manuscript.

Place	Date	Hour	Summary of Events and Information	Remarks and references to Appendices
CLAIREFAYE	1/7/15	9 a.m.	A car of umpires drove among the contents. The man listed on the card 15th in Greenwich. He has been reported in a similar depth under observation.	See vis Sheet 12
		10 a.m.	The Sam. 16th Batt. arrived & transferred the truck & have now paid up the care of Meusen.	"
		4 p.m.	Visited the Officers Mess, Rest Station, and cemeteries.	"
	2/7/15	10. a.m.	The Superior, 1 Capture, 1 Lieut. arrived in reinforcement. Taken in 15th Straing 18. On departure in substituting care.	"
		3 p.m.	Pains in vampa. S the arrange of motor ambulances with the 10. R.A.	"
		4 p.m.	LIEUT. BARTON reported to C.R.E.'s office as joint ambulance to the Can. & Supp. McCARTHY also on high to lock this through the hand.	"
		"	Very wet all day.	
	3/7/15	9 a.m.	Art. Park are coming keep. Could not arrive with Supervision.	
	3/7/15	"	do motor the place any supply.	
		2 p.m.	Paid visit A. Sedlic - Sent money. C. Freeli. 15 Reg. met MATISON ROCLAND for exchange with	
	4/7/15	9. a.m.	Sent to Motor Ambulance at MATISON ROCLAND for exchange with	
			8/10 R.A.	
			the Mr. T. Superior returned & stated that 8/10 R.A. had no orders	
	"	6 p.m.	to and any care away. Reported this to Colours. Left with my own car.	

WAR DIARY
or
INTELLIGENCE SUMMARY
(Erase heading not required.)

Army Form C. 2118

Instructions regarding War Diaries and Intelligence Summaries are contained in F. S. Regs, Part II. and the Staff Manual respectively. Title Pages will be prepared in manuscript.

Place	Date	Hour	Summary of Events and Information	Remarks and references to Appendices
CLAIR MARAIS	4/12/15	10.30 am	4 cars from N⁰ 10 F. Amb. arrived in entrepot.	
	5/12/15	9. am	Supt. Off. rum'd to Camp. 6 – N⁰ 10. F.A. And the two arrived in entrepot.	
	"	11. am	S.M. McATEER & Sgt. LEONARD went to N⁰ 10 N.J.A. to give in names to Mr FODEN transfers and did not return – identified no orderlies and reported no bag outfitting –	
do.	6/12/15	3.30 pm 11. am	D.D.M.S. N⁰ 1 – Corps (Colonel SWAN) visited the Our Officers and went over the units on a fair day & fixing rooms	
do.	7/12/15	10. am	One of the heavy lorries drove did during the night – Reported on bring officer. Was sent to the Tr. avenue and had a foot in it. Time in the morning, he was being seen to in the afternoon. Visited Qrm. Stevin.	
do.	8/12/15	11. am 12.30 pm	Arrived. Received orders re entrepot of Auction – P. C. Receive to return two & A.C.F. C. H/11.A.A. Sent to N⁰ 12. F.A.	
do.	9/12/15	10. am 10.30 " 11. am 11.30 "	C. Section arrived from N⁰ 12. R. Am. became. Sect N⁰ 12.F.A. rep. to N⁰ 12. F.A. R. sect. arrived from N⁰ 11. F. Amb. to Back. Bat. to ACHEUX. Supt. S⁰ & men	

Army Form C. 2118

WAR DIARY
or
INTELLIGENCE SUMMARY
(Erase heading not required.)

Instructions regarding War Diaries and Intelligence Summaries are contained in F. S. Regs., Part II. and the Staff Manual respectively. Title Pages will be prepared in manuscript.

Place	Date	Hour	Summary of Events and Information	Remarks and references to Appendices
BLAIR FAYE	9/1/15	2 pm	A. Section left to reconnoitre via D 2/11 F.A. to PATRICK and Lieut HAY went via Pondic. Very wet all day.	Reunion Appx 112
do	"	6 pm	2 Reconnoitring cars arrived from No. 20 F.A.	"
do	10/1/15	9 am	Heavy details of D 2/11 F.A. returned to rest bivouac. Handed over section from the position to 1st Batn on A.C.H.S.U.T	"
	"	10 am	Sent 30 men & D 2/11 F.A. section in advance of C. Reunion	"
	"	2 pm	B Section of D 2/11 F.A. relieved 11/7 F.A. section of "– 2nd Batn –	"
	"	5 pm	Remainder of B sect 11/7 F.A. – Out of line –	
do	11/2	11 am	Advg section Pondic to Reunion. Commander 6 pm station from Intercom here in part team of Pondic.	
do	12/2	2 pm	Observed presents – All counter	
	"	6 pm	Paris – via – L- Officers. Reconnoitred.	
	13/2	9 am	First Inspn – Reconnoitring –	
	"	2 pm	Sent conversation men to observe arrivals arrived –	
	"	3 pm	Visit from orderlies	
	14/2	10 am	Lieuts G were ordered, on duty very warm	
	"	10.30	Lieuts G were D and O.S. reporting back the personnel large number of men are ready to work, and they are ready to protect them from the Germans.	
	"	2.30	Lieut G to receive the Germans	
	"	6 pm	Remained that morning at detachment 2 Officers to represent – One section	

WAR DIARY
or
INTELLIGENCE SUMMARY
(Erase heading not required.)

Army Form C. 2118

Instructions regarding War Diaries and Intelligence Summaries are contained in F. S. Regs., Part II. and the Staff Manual respectively. Title Pages will be prepared in manuscript.

Place	Date	Hour	Summary of Events and Information	Remarks and references to Appendices
CLAIRFAYE	14/2/15		M.O. of the 8º N.I.R. and one to relieve M.O. of the 9º N.I.R.	
	15/2/15	9 am	Detail Lieut. R.B. PURCE to relieve Lieut. LEE. of the 9º N.I.R. at VARENNES. He is to proceed —	
"			Detail Capt. T. GRIMSON to relieve Lieut. BLAIR of the 9º N.I.R. He is to use up his details into the Battn. arms out of the interior; Rank may cause inroad. Men in his hands deliver to him the inspection — It needs getting. Had to put and early delivery. Very odd —	
"	16/2/15	3pm	Dressing Boot Station.	
	17/2/15	9.am	Review arrange for an interview to 6º ENGLEBELLMAR & 6º AMIENS. Parties went on ambulance armed on or parade.	
"		10. am	Arrived at Paris — In question. Inspection. Next détail. Very short & neat.	
		3.30	Paid out the S.O.C. 4º Div. his Ambulance.	
	18/2/15	10. am	Capt. T. GRIMSON proceeded to FORCEVILLES to take over district ambulance.	
"		11.30 am	of 9º N.I.R. — Arrived orders and orders.	
		3 pm	A.R.M.O. cannot send order.	
		4 pm	Orders to R.G. BLAIR.	
		6 pm	Brigade arriving — him orders to try for the 9º N.I.R.	
	19/2/15	9. am	Sent Capt. O'NEIL to relieve Capt. EMERSON who is proceed on leave.	
"		11 am		

WAR DIARY
or
INTELLIGENCE SUMMARY
(Erase heading not required.)

Army Form C. 2118

Instructions regarding War Diaries and Intelligence Summaries are contained in F. S. Regs., Part II. and the Staff Manual respectively. Title Pages will be prepared in manuscript.

Place	Date	Hour	Summary of Events and Information	Remarks and references to Appendices
CLAIRFAYE	20/2/15	9 am	Capt EMERSON - proceed on 14 days leave.	Appendices
"	21/2/15	2.15 pm	Shoot 100 mm L.F. Batt. at ACHEUX. Detonation of F.C 1110 = P.A. on hour meeting F.C Shrike. Batt. Shoot Confirmed report of actions on R.M.S. Wilson with a view to his Muirnt Lt Dowse Rink. Artillery orders and instns. R.M.S. Wilson.	"
"	22/2/15	11 am	Had an interview of sent for Lerind.	
"	23/2/15	2.15 pm	Rec'd wire of the President of Medical Board assembling on the 26 - Lt examine men of Nevers Corps. Detailed Lt. BLAIR as a member -	
		11 am	Lt examine men of Nevers Corps.	
			Intervenn -	
"	"	3 pm	Orders arrived C and H BLISS 11th F.A. to proceed with the 12th F. Arct. on the 26th	
"	24/2/15	8 pm	Attend visit Joint Staff.	
"	25/2/15	12 m.	Then drive of division - the G.O.C. + Div Orders - The men at Runu.	
"	"	2 pm	Attn - various Officers Joint Staff.	
"	26/2/15	9 am	Medical Board Lt examine men of the 12th F. Arct. on presiding Capt. Transports leave on 6.00 pm	

WAR DIARY
or
INTELLIGENCE SUMMARY
(Erase heading not required.)

Army Form C. 2118

Instructions regarding War Diaries and Intelligence Summaries are contained in F. S. Regs., Part II. and the Staff Manual respectively. Title Pages will be prepared in manuscript.

Place	Date	Hour	Summary of Events and Information	Remarks and references to Appendices
BLAIRFAYE	26/12	7 pm	Returns from Amiens Road — Capt HARVEY. 11:15 7.A. arrived in relief of Lts BLISS.	AMIENS
"	27/12	9 am	went to MAILLY & prisoners of Divine Camp. Returns to H.Q. premises. Orders rec'd to decide on Officer for let piquet duty w/54th Brit. Am. Comn. at BLAIR details:—	—
"	28/12	11 am	Lt on Guy Orders 36 = Dvrs; Mgs: 683. Sgt 1774 Da Sirva party to visite: — 6 — Pte 110 = Q. Aulett. Trim. Corp 3 — Evans —	—
"	—	3 pm	of visit BLISS dept. to join Pte 12 = Q.A.	—
"	—	4:30 pm	of visit BLAIR dept. to join Pte Am. Comn. on let piquet duty =	—
"	29/12	2:15 pm	Snack in mess 6 — 15 Battn at ACHEUX.	—
"	—	2:30 pm	Visit from a friend	—
"	30/12	2 pm	Visit from a friend	—
"	"	2 pm	activated American transport arm in ACHEUX & phoned the Hure on Road	—
"	31/12	9 am	—	—
"	"	12 m	Previous from Amiens Road	—
"	"	2:15 pm	Parc, Pte Evans first MELLIS (sick) appointing Arlenn Poris — arrives in	1
"	"	4 pm	Mgs. Genett accompanying the Open States & men & officer visit North Prairie —	
			R.14 seen driver back 11.00 Ft Aurbland ont 11.15	

Confidential

War Diary

7TH 110 Field Ambulance R.A.M.C

From 1st January 1916 to 31st January 1916

WAR DIARY
or
INTELLIGENCE SUMMARY
(Erase heading not required.)

Army Form C. 2118

Instructions regarding War Diaries and Intelligence Summaries are contained in F.S. Regs., Part II. and the Staff Manual respectively. Title Pages will be prepared in manuscript.

Place	Date	Hour	Summary of Events and Information	Remarks and references to Appendices
CLAIRFAYE	1/7/16	9. am	One of the heavy Troop Lorries has but arrived from Clair. Reports to the Veterinary office was advised to hand back to firm munition.	—
"	2/7/16	9. am	Received instructions and wagon repairing the remounts & horses sent by rail from ACHEUX. To the upper than the 3 horses.	—
"	3/7/16	3 pm	Arduous enemies most dates, arranged for conveying mules and to refused remainder of personnel in more schemes. Later orders being than 6/7/16. The order new to reporting the receipt of A. needs of No.11 R.A.) The relief of the No.11 G.A. occurs to the H.Q.	)
"	4/7/16	4 pm		)
"		9. am	Capt N.C. PATRICK proceeded on 14 days leave this morning the morning relief of Capt J. EWING of the No.12 morning to proceed. his accretion having expired.	)
"		10. am	He relief of No.11 F.A. Capt to again H.Q. under Capt HARVEY.	—
"		11.30 am	A Senior No.12 G.A. advised from 9 & No.2.A. having finished its period of attachment for training.	—
"	5/7/16	10 am	Capt EMERSON- returned from leave.	—
"	"	12 m	The A.R.M.G. & from War Army, Veterinary officer weeks the new establ.	—
"	6/7/16	3 pm	John Than arrival and explained the ordinary of the D.M.S. Sent- party of 10 men to the Baths at ACHEUX.	—
"	7/7/16	4 pm	Visit from England.	—
		10. pm	Recording 6-12 m.O. much J.F.S. Leyson go private law and were keep on	—

WAR DIARY
or
INTELLIGENCE SUMMARY
(Erase heading not required.)

Army Form C. 2118

Instructions regarding War Diaries and Intelligence Summaries are contained in F.S. Regs., Part II. and the Staff Manual respectively. Title Pages will be prepared in manuscript.

Place	Date	Hour	Summary of Events and Information	Remarks and references to Appendices
BLAIR PAYE	8/16	10 am	Visit from Arens.	
"	9/16	10 am	Sent an M.O. to visit a French soldier on leaving HARPONVILLE to apres	
			Lt. opposing from Arens.	
		4 pm	Lieut BLAIR received from lit. passing dug out est to D.A.C.	
			Sent Motor Ambulance to AMIENS with French Drivers one Hospital	
"	10.16	10 am	3,3,0. reports to be carried to uniforms & issues in Army.	
		11 am	Visit from Arens	
		3 pm	Sent one O.S. 1.4 pm to D.1.2 Cas Base in connection with systems	
			& bringing up supplies from Noidens by means of horse transport.	
		6 pm	Lieut A. CLIMIE & Lieut J.F. LAMBIE reported to	
		6 am	[Lt.] Duty & later on the strong to.	
	11/16	5 pm	Orders received to detach a M.O. to review Col. GRIMSON marking	
			on our —	
	12/16	6 pm	Instructed Capt. O'NEILL to proceed to VARENNES & review	
			Col. GRIMSON	
	13/16	10 am	Sent Lieut. HAY to take an charge of officer' room Field in	

WAR DIARY
or
INTELLIGENCE SUMMARY
(Erase heading not required.)

Army Form C. 2118

Place	Date	Hour	Summary of Events and Information	Remarks and references to Appendices
CLAIR FAYE	13/6	4 pm	Orders rec'd appointing A/C PRYDE O/C Serjeant & N.C.O's I/C M.T. transport	
"	14/6	9 am	Rept. M.T. Ann. between C- 9-12 Z.A. & 7 Tan Cars & Log & paris	
			C-VILLERS BOCAGE	
		10 am	Visiting Officers Pom Stern	
		10.0	Orders re's Officers' Pom Stern & a.v a. Amb. Pom Stern	
		3 pm	Paid men & tr inspectn of transport	
	16/6	9 am	Paraded on time — Capt EMERSON assumed command during my absence	
			13.14 seen Divr. ing. General	
	"	2-15 pm	Church Parade — United Service at E Emifaye by Rev. Williamson C.F.S.	
	17/6 12 noon	Heavy draught Horses purchased B/ from rich. discharged by order of Lt. W. Anderson A.V.C.	
		6-30 pm	Evacuated from Officers Rest Station Capt. Cox 1st Royal Warwicks to Highland C.C.S. at Villers Bocage as cases of "Encephalitis Lethargica".	
	18/6	9 am	Privates Hopkins & Hanley M.T. proceeded on 8 days leave this morning.	
		10 am	Reptn of Motor ambulance fromgn J. Ilenborger having been held up on the road owing to breakdown. Saw C. Hospitals personnel. Rpted his arrival for duty.	
		3 pm	General Alinson Field & Col Reilly HQ. boarded the Rest Station. Inspected them round and expressed the working of the D.R.S.	

WAR DIARY
or
INTELLIGENCE SUMMARY
(Erase heading not required.)

Army Form C. 2118

Place	Date	Hour	Summary of Events and Information	Remarks and references to Appendices
Elverdinghe	19/6	11 am	A.D.M.S. visited D.R.S.	
"	"	4.15 pm	Lieut. J. R. Forbes reported his arrival for duty with the 110 F. A.	
"	20/6	2.15 pm	Detailed Lt. Blair to proceed to 10th Royal Irish Rifles to take over temporary medical charge and Lieut. Bulletin going on leave	
"	"	4 pm	Visit from A.D.M.S.	
"	"	10 pm	Capt. Patrick reported his arrival from fortnight's leave.	
"	21/6	9 am	One Warrant Officer and six men proceeded on leave this morning.	
"	"	4 pm	A.D.M.S. visited Officers Rest Station	
"	"	6 pm	Visited Officers Rest Station	
"	22/6	10 am	Memorial Polin proceeded to 11th F. Amb. for temporary duty. (Authority from A.D.M.S. 23rd Jany.)	
"	23/6	11.45 am	A.D.M.S. visited D.R.S.	
"	"	11.45 am	Col. Given D.M.S. & Corps visited D.R.S.	
"	"	5 pm	Detailed Lieut. Blair to proceed to 2nd Irish Regiment to take over temporary medical charge B/fn Batt.e. vice Capt. Raffle R.A.M.C. proceeding on leave (Authority - Telegram A.D.M.S.)	
"	25/6	9 am	Lt Blair & Capt. Raffle proceeded on leave this morning	
"	"	10 am	Detailed Lieut. Pemble and Reid for the to proceed to Div Conference at Peelvoorvoerd at 11 am (Technical advice to 3rd Army press) (Instructions received from A.D.M.S.)	
"	26/6	4 pm	A.D.M.S. visited D.R.S.	
"	"	10 pm	Returned f/t leave.	
"	27/6	9 am	Received command of 16 R.A.	
"	"	4 pm	Re G.O.C. 4 = Divisions views and others	
"	28/6	4 pm	Cap: EMERSON reverses C. Officers DM's = M.O. etc, returns Dtd. Lieut. HAYES to relieve ofr CORKEY proceeding on leave on Europe.	

WAR DIARY
or
INTELLIGENCE SUMMARY

(Erase heading not required.)

Army Form C. 2118

Place	Date	Hour	Summary of Events and Information	Remarks and references to Appendices
BLAIRFAYE	28/10	3 p.m.	Pay out and too Helmet Inspection -	
"	30/10	3 p.m.	Arthur's visit - ours 65st & Gordon visit - 1st News of 1st Division -	
"	31/10	10 a.m.	Went to MONDICOURT to see press proposed pt. + pure street -	
		4 p.m.	Nelwn? went to Arthur to reports - Arthur informed me that the 11St his Ambulance in replacing the 86 = Divis. & are emergency - down the news on enemies.	

13.14 Week Duncan
Off. a. Naurul
O.C. 110 Field Ambulance

4th DD. to be 1. Feb.1916
31st " from " " "

No. 110 Field Ambulance.

Feb 19 1916

War Diary
110th Field Ambulance. R.A.M.C.

from Feb 1 to Feb 29th 1916

110. F.A.
36th Div
Vol 5.

Army Form C. 2118

WAR DIARY
or
INTELLIGENCE SUMMARY
(Erase heading not required.)

Instructions regarding War Diaries and Intelligence Summaries are contained in F. S. Regs., Part II. and the Staff Manual respectively. Title Pages will be prepared in manuscript.

Place	Date	Hour	Summary of Events and Information	Remarks and references to Appendices
CHAIRFAY=	1/7/6	10.am	Orders to div. from — wires and ammn/ld arms for necessary to certain advance states to the division.	
		11.am	DD in S y= Capn & DD in S 14= Capns good in wait — Shed these round to places.	
		1 pm	St. Stenbers 75= Bdr. arrived to arrange wires to 110= 2 Bdr. agreeing to division.	
	2/7/6	6.am	Capn O'NEIL & 2 men proceed on leave. S.M. LOWRIE & Spr. ORTEN-obs & rejoind = div. from S.M. RUSSELL & Spr. HARDY report to 110= 2 Bde & Sec certain movement S/I by amb. lorries to MON DE COURT.	
˝		9.am	1 N.c.o & 3 men in charge of — a.m. orders from — division.	
˝		11.am	Various Officers from Stations visits to pataik & susic to proceed to HAILEY=MAILLET	
˝		3 pm	Ordered wires & Lasic Ionning Stall for Bj=11 2 Bde & 6 ten men	
˝		5 pm	Detained B. Sect. — under Capt PATRICK, & Lieut FORBES. Lorries — two ambulances to proceed to COLIN CAMPS to accompany	
	3/7/6	4. am	troops to the 4= div on the move. B. Section left to 7 ten men Dunning Staill in MAICEY.	
		11.30 am	Visit from Askind. One ear of explosives vans taken to	
˝		3 pm	Visit from Askind. One end of explosives vans taken to Sta. Lt. & Suing Bathan.	

WAR DIARY or INTELLIGENCE SUMMARY

Army Form C. 2118

Place	Date	Hour	Summary of Events and Information	Remarks and references to Appendices
CLAIRFAYE	3/7/16	3pm	Lieut CLIMIE returned from his army buys. Saw Capt EMERSON & MAILLY to relieve Capt PATRICK who	
"	4/7/16	9 am	the latter went to DOUCLENS to give evidence on a Court Martial	
		3pm	Capt EMERSON returned from MAILLY	
"	5/7/16	9.30 am	Paid a visit to Dummy Street at MAILLY. Six men arrived as reinforcements	
		3pm	Detailed 2Lt LAMBIE, 1 NCO & 6 men to proceed to Dummy Street at MESNIC tomorrow to relieve one from the 12 F.A.	
			Am Lt CLIMIE 1 NCO & 20 men to proceed to MAILLY & report to Capt Patrick	
			Jeans returns for Capt PATRICK to return 18/prem 1 NCO & 24	
"	6/7/16	8 am	men to the men entered Dummy Street at AUCHONVILLERS	
			MESNIC party left 8.15 am morning also the MAILLY party	
		10 am	Emerson & one car of men to Highland C.C.S.	
			Detailed one car of men to proceed to HAMEL & occupy an inn	
			they are there	
		5.30 pm	One mr/s ambulance to proceed to HAMEL to evacuate wounded.	
"	9/7/16	9 am	Rejoins the 36 Div. the lorries came up to relieve the 4th Div.

WAR DIARY
or
INTELLIGENCE SUMMARY

(Erase heading not required.)

Army Form C. 2118

Instructions regarding War Diaries and Intelligence Summaries are contained in F.S. Regs., Part II. and the Staff Manual respectively. Title Pages will be prepared in manuscript.

Place	Date	Hour	Summary of Events and Information	Remarks and references to Appendices
BLAIR PAYE	7/7/16	3pm	Returned to Div. from a visit to the Fd. Ambulances	
"	"	5pm	Capt. BLAIR returned from temporary duty. Ordered revisit the studio on presence in MAIZEY is the attended to Fr. 108. 2 But. as a temporary measure. Record orders accordingly.	
"	8/7/16	10am	Visit from Divisional	
"	"	3pm	Visit from O.C. 2 Coy A.S.C.	
"	9/7/16	3pm	Return LAMBIE's Fr. Signal on MESNIL relieved today	
"	"	4pm	Send from HAMEL reliving to his Entents.	
"	10/7/16	11am	The Corps 36: Div. visited the D.R.S. His C-in-C Officer Post Station	
"	11/7/16	10am	Return 76: Div. inspected the DRS.	
"	12/7/16	4pm	Visit Officer Divi Train. Only one officer in.	
"	13/7/16	6am	Lieut HAY proceed on Escort Pre: interpretr. escort of Cars	
"	"	10am	O.C. 2.A.W.V. Count C. Exempt.	
"	"	11.30am	Escort comprises 6-own 1 NCOs 112 horses as a covering party to VANCHELLES 4	
"	14/7/16	6am	Sent 3 Cars 6-N210 2.A. + 3 Cars for 8210 2.A. arrived.	
"	"	3pm	D.D.M.S. 17 Corps to his Quan. States to Adm. Offin. Pont Statims	
"	"	6pm	Quick from FORBES Quick from MAIZEY - Sent to Offin Pont Statims.	

1875 Wt. W593/826 1,000,000 4/15 J.B.C. & A. A.D.S.S./Forms/C. 2118.

WAR DIARY
or
INTELLIGENCE SUMMARY.
(Erase heading not required.)

Army Form C. 2118.

Place	Date	Hour	Summary of Events and Information	Remarks and references to Appendices
LAIRFAYE	15/7/16	9 am	Detained 1 NCO & 11 men for duty in the Brait. Batt ACHEUX. Captain EMERSON detained as O.C. on a temporary manner.	
"		11 am	Orders under Runt Steen, also offices, Runt Steen.	
"	16/15	1 am	Day am & strongly shelling enemy's lines.	
"	17/7/16	9 am	Detained Capt R.G. BLAIR to receive Sligt PURCE as M.O. & 8th D.O.R. while the later proceeds on leave.	
"		3 pm	Message received & re-write Lt. PURCE 10/oy.R – Capt BLAIR reports sick to detailed Lt. LAYSILL as his to be temper. asst. madg.	
"		10 am	Capt O'NEIL returned off leave.	
"	18/7/16	3 pm	Received S.O. 107: Bde. re Sapper, Stores –	
"		5 pm	Lieut & 50 Orr. R.M.O. as inspection of 4th Bye CROZIER 9th R.I.R.	
"	19/7/16	12 m	Lient received from M.H.Q. on being received by 1st P.R.R.	
"		6 pm	Very heavy bombardment Stars. On final one man to bivouac & to ready in coal of company.	
"	20/7/16	9 am	Sent 6 Heavy Drayer horses to FORCEVILLE to report to Dr. from R.T. Officers under Runt Steen.	
"		12 m		

WAR DIARY
or
INTELLIGENCE SUMMARY.
(Erase heading not required.)

Army Form C. 2118.

Place	Date	Hour	Summary of Events and Information	Remarks and references to Appendices
PLAINFAYE	20/7/16	8.30 am	Scout 3 Ed. began to VAUCHELLES to run troops from 46 Div.	
"	"	11 am	Motor recce for above arrived to hire & assist in addition to transport the 100 of morning. Motor ambulances assisting eg.	
"	22/7/16	4 pm	Units from DOULLENS.	
"	23/7/16	2 pm	Pass am. orders received am MAILLY.	
"	"	5.30 pm	Sudden orders received to move to BEAUVAL on the 29th Inst.	
"	"	10 pm	Lieut HAY arrived off leave.	
"	24/7/16	9 am	Scout Lieut HAY to report to advanced pty on duty at the Baths.	
"	"	11 am	Scout orders received to say that to move is postponed for 3 days.	
"	"	12 h	Lieut FORBES from off the aid out & relieves him for duty.	
"	"	6 pm	Capt. EMERSON receives C. Officer Pers' orders to duty.	
"	25/7/16	10 am	Capt. EMERSON proceeds on the aid out & returns to Officer New Field.	
"	"	-	Lt FORBES am. C. Officer and proc on temporary duty.	
"	"	-	Very busy time of season.	
"	26/7/16	10 am	Divies Officers' Rev Field, have the various Field units to are DOCTORS.	
"	"	-	7 Gen. El. 5 Cp. R. E.	

WAR DIARY
or
INTELLIGENCE SUMMARY.
(Erase heading not required.)

Army Form C. 2118.

Place	Date	Hour	Summary of Events and Information	Remarks and references to Appendices
CLAIRFAYE	27/16	9 am	Win arrived "THAN".	
		10 am	Destroying officer unspecified turned	
	28/16	10 am	Cpl BURTON francs army Depot with Pay. Orders received 6 and Sgt. KIRWAN & Asroun to bug on leave.	
		3 pm	13 man from 1st N.I.n. arrived to dusts Leicester	
	29/16	10 am	Sgt KIRWAN proceed to Asroun to bug. Cpt HALLIDAY and in escort.	
			Sent man to 1st N.I.n. 6 Vaccinates to be seen by Dentist. Capt EMERSON taken off the sick enlist Lieut FORBES receives him to duty.	

R H Jean Duncan
Lieut. Cornel Rame
O.C. 110th Sat. Ambrun

36th Div A.7.6 2118

War Diary **Confidential** 110/7
110th Field Ambulance R.A.M.C. Amb
B.E.F. Vol 6

From 1st March 1916 To 31st March 1916

Vol 6

COMMITTEE FOR THE
MEDICAL HISTORY OF THE WAR
Date 9 – JUN. 1915

WAR DIARY
or
INTELLIGENCE SUMMARY.
(Erase heading not required.)

Army Form C. 2118.

Place	Date	Hour	Summary of Events and Information	Remarks and references to Appendices
BLAIRFAY	1/3/16	6 pm	Orders received to act Estain - accompanied by Capt GREEN departing	
		7 pm	Lieut LAMBIE, relieved from company duty will to C.O.O.R.	
		3 pm	Handed St mm w/E 15 over Pris Lyptus Detain.	
	2/16	4 pm	Pte Pte. MORRIS w/s pts 6-15 under arrest.	
			Pairs sent to Dr SMITHING who is accused of fraudulent enrolment. Read him to clear arrest.	
	1/16		doing exam	
	3/16	3 pm	actions in prisoners to various Officers. Prs'd. opines when in newspaper of the civic. Betting pounds.	
	4/16	10 am	For Robinson come here, asked me to propose to him in 100 extra presents - hunts concepts everything -	
		5 pm	Orly arm - so exam amid.	
	5/16	2 pm	Church parade - Lieut & Dr SWAINE hypnosed w/16. R.G. Let to Alamein custom forward regiment.	
	6/16	9 am	Recd 15 Ops MITCHELL attached to the R.G. to the Officer Part Stain.	

WAR DIARY
or
INTELLIGENCE SUMMARY.
(Erase heading not required.)

Army Form C. 2118.

Place	Date	Hour	Summary of Events and Information	Remarks and references to Appendices
CLAIRFAYE	7/16	2.15pm	O.C. No. 2 Coy A.S.C. inspects horses & transports.	
"	8/16	12 n	Issued new equipment and P.H. for horses.	
"	"	2 pm	S.M. BATSON M.S.C. arrived in receipt of J.M. RUSSELL A.S.C.	
"	9/16	—	Nothing to note.	
"	10/16	2 pm	Inspects & serviced with the new equipment.	
"	"	3.00	Attended conference on the arms officer.	
"	"	5 pm	Lectured all R.G. BLAIR & mine qted. COMPLETED in aid air-no. movie 193 Bde N.F.A.	
"	11/16	"	S & hrs 10th Cabn & Arduno inspect. to not finish.	
"	12/16	2.12 h	Church parade.	
"	13/16	3 pm	Inspects B. Sect in new equipment.	
"	"	5.00h	Lectured to men with the arms instructor.	
"	14/16	2 pm	Gas helmet drill.	
"	"	4 pm	A.R.M.S. pays a visit. Most Frai. the Ren. D.R. MITCHELL. Then	
"	"	"	rft duties train & reports J. Buel C.	
"	15/16	9 am	Capt BLAIR posts promoted 6th 15th MAY 1725 By R.F.A. list H. CAMPBELL	

WAR DIARY
or
INTELLIGENCE SUMMARY.
(Erase heading not required.)

Army Form C. 2118.

Place	Date	Hour	Summary of Events and Information	Remarks and references to Appendices
LAIRFAYE	17/3/16	3 pm	Attached in France in the hearing office.	
"	18/3/16	4 pm	Asting visits not attached but not arrived; are more of the present.	
"	20/3/16	4 pm	Prs 4th Army visits an inspector of the Offices Mess Acers) of the Sergt. Non-Acers.	
"	21/3/16	9 am	One NCO & 1 man proceeded on leave.	
"	22/3/16	11.30 am	One cas & minor moment to No. 4 C.C.S. Lieut to Lieut Campbell R. Burns moment to B.J & C.C.S. (P.U.O.)	
"	23/3/16	10 am	Visit from Deveroy & D.DO(2).	
"	"	3 pm	One NCO proceeded on leave.	
"	24/3/16	11 am	One car & Seven horses sent to No.4 C.C.S.	
"	"	3 pm	3 men admit to reinforcement.	
"	25/3/16	10 am	Lt. Campbell R. Burns, reports to duty from No. 4 C.C.S.	
"	"	3 pm	Lt. Campbell again sent in out cite with influenza.	
"	26/3/16	4 pm	Lt. Campbell moment to B.J.4 C.C.S. (P.U.O.) reports to the division.	
"	"		Return. Such when received as more of the division.	
"	27/3/16	11 am	Attend division and station again & received 2 menuto & one 2 rolled.	

WAR DIARY
or
INTELLIGENCE SUMMARY.
(Erase heading not required.)

Army Form C. 2118.

Place	Date	Hour	Summary of Events and Information	Remarks and references to Appendices
CLAIRFAYE	27/6	10 am	The Revd. MORRIS proceeded on leave – also Sgt. 14 & 2 Dy H.R.	
"	28/6	3.30	Critical confuns to Evening office.	
"	"	4 pm	Union offices pro priors.	
"	29/6	10 am	Lt. BURROWS R. Army reports his arrival for duty.	
"	30/6	11 am	Sgt. wait rest scheme	
"	"	6 pm	wire 6° arrows 6° up members for out officers wires 6.10.	
"	31	10 am	Visit from arrows	

B.H. Sellers Drunken
Lt. Col. Naver
O.C. No: 2nd Ambulance

Confidential

36th Div.   110 F Amb.
           Vol 7

War Diary
of
110th Field Ambulance R.A.M.C.

from April 1st 1916 to April 30th 1916

Volume 7

COMMITTEE FOR THE
MEDICAL HISTORY OF THE WAR
Date   9 – JUN. 1916

Army Form C. 2118.

WAR DIARY
or
INTELLIGENCE SUMMARY.
(Erase heading not required.)

Instructions regarding War Diaries and Intelligence Summaries are contained in F. S. Regs., Part II. and the Staff Manual respectively. Title pages will be prepared in manuscript.

Place	Date	Hour	Summary of Events and Information	Remarks and references to Appendices
CLAIR FAYE	1/16	5.pm	1 NCO & 1 man proceeded on leave to 9 Corps.	
"	2/16	9 am	Lt. CLIMIE proceeds to relieve M.O. of 36 D AC which on leave.	
"	3/16	3.30	Attended Conference at Arseuil Officine.	
		5.7pm	Lt CLIMIE returned from 36 D.A.C. as there is been appointed the M.O.	
			Pope will not proceed on leave.	
"	4/16	3pm	Point arm	
"	5/16	2 pm	Been with Doctors over the front line & wire up the scheme for evacuation of causalities line 6 HAMEL, THIEPVAL & HAMOUILLE. Peuren	
			at 7 pm.	
"	6/16	9.am	Lt CLIMIE proceeded to PUCHVILLERS.	
			Visit from Doctors	
"	7/16	6 pm	Lt HAY and attachment from the Battn returned to H.Q. 15 Day.	
"	8/16	3.45pm	Received one Scout desirephets of men at OR8.	
"	9/16	10 am	8 Other NCOs & 3 men proceeded on leave Intigans.	
"		2pm	Attended conference at advance of VARENNES. for Divisions Scheme	
"	10 & 3.30 pm		of evacuation of wounded from the line.	

1577 Wt. W10791/1773 500,000 1/15 D. D. & L. A.D.S.S./Forms/C. 2118.

WAR DIARY
or
INTELLIGENCE SUMMARY.
(Erase heading not required.)

Army Form C. 2118.

Instructions regarding War Diaries and Intelligence Summaries are contained in F. S. Regs., Part II. and the Staff Manual respectively. Title pages will be prepared in manuscript.

Place	Date	Hour	Summary of Events and Information	Remarks and references to Appendices
LAHIRIAPUR	11/6	4.30 h	Proceeded on leave. Capt. EMERSON i/c adm. in my absence.	
"	12/6	12.m	D. clearing visited and inspected.	B.1st Seam Brown M.O. in
"	"	6 h.m	Visited Officers Mess & Field.	
"	13/6	3 h.m	Sick visit & several men in camp to evacuate.	
"	14/6	3.30 h	Arrangements & wants not known.	
"	15/6	12.n	Arrangements in progress not known.	
"	16/6	11.am	D. clears & Cooks visited and refreshed. Inspected the rooms & the inspected.	
"	"	-	Also inspected Packing & receiving High foods.	
"	18/6	12 n	C. O. visited from camp as being evacuated by arrangements.	
				H. Ameron Capt Remc
"	18/6	12 n	Return from leave having been recalled.	
"	"	3 h.m	Received instructions from Advance to prepare an establish camp.	
"	"	-	to take in all cases of Enteron diseases in the Div'n.	
"	19/6	9.am	Started arrangement of an isolated Camp in the grounds.	
"	20/6	3 h.m	Capt EMERSON & Capt O'NEILL sent to the front line as from the above prepared for evacuation.	

WAR DIARY
or
INTELLIGENCE SUMMARY.

(Erase heading not required.)

Army Form C. 2118.

Instructions regarding War Diaries and Intelligence Summaries are contained in F. S. Regs., Part II. and the Staff Manual respectively. Title pages will be prepared in manuscript.

Place	Date	Hour	Summary of Events and Information	Remarks and references to Appendices
BLAIRFAYE	21/7/16	9 am	Three new recruits arrived yesterday evening — also 1 Sgt & 1 man as reinforcement.	
	22/7/16	10 am	Detailed Lt. HAY to duty in the Remount.	
	Sat 23/7/16	—	Event Monday, Tuesday, Spent —	
	25/7/16	9 am	Rations Lt. LAM sick 15 French Lt. VARENNES & noted M.O. is PM promising on leave. Stored horses their camp for Remnant horses. Archived confirmation to posting officer.	
		3.30	DADVS & Colo came in re Glanders & arranged to take samples being supplied.	
	26/7/16	10 am	Owens 10 Morphine to sick remounts Arenes, Donkeys sick.	
	27/7/16	12 m		
	28/7/16	10 am	Morgue visits 6' day 5' office & 10 O.R. were arriving here in men Contracts. Kit & Arrange a remount & notice; this is in connection c/t taining & the numen contract are a Kriss ? Made arrangement accordingly.	
	28/7/16	11.30 am	One officer & 10 men (Mounted contracts) arrived.	

WAR DIARY
or
INTELLIGENCE SUMMARY.

(Erase heading not required.)

Army Form C. 2118.

Instructions regarding War Diaries and Intelligence Summaries are contained in F. S. Regs., Part II. and the Staff Manual respectively. Title pages will be prepared in manuscript.

Place	Date	Hour	Summary of Events and Information	Remarks and references to Appendices
Blanfaye	28/7/18	3-1.15 pm	C.O. - Lt-Col Sudlow proceeded on leave. Capt Emerson assuming Command J/11078	
		3.30 pm	G.S.O.I. 3d " Div? - Lt-Col Plair visited the Camp.	
	29/7/18	11.30 am	Two Officers + 105 men 9th Inniskillings (Advance Parties) arrived.	
		4 pm	A.D.M.S. 26th Div? visited the Camp & made an inspection.	
	30 "		Continued increasing accommodation of Camp by erecting Marquees + increasing size of kitchen.	

H Emerson Capt R.A.M.C.
for O.C. 110°

8/9/18

110 F Amb
Vol 8
36th Div

WAR DIARY
110th FIELD AMBULANCE

From May 1st 1916 To May 31st 1916.

Volume VIII

COMMITTEE FOR THE
MEDICAL HISTORY OF THE WAR
Date 26 JUN 1915

CONFIDENTIAL
110 Field Ambulance

WAR DIARY or INTELLIGENCE SUMMARY

Army Form C. 2118.

Place	Date	Hour	Summary of Events and Information	Remarks and references to Appendices
Chocques	28/7	3.15 p	C.O. went on leave. Capt. Emerson assuming command of 110 F.A.	
		3.30 p	G.S.O.I. Lt-Col Plaine visited the Camp.	
	29/7	11.30 a	Four Officers + 105 men 9th Inniskillings (Measles Contacts) arrived	
		4 pm	A.D.M.S. Col Grey visited the Camp & inspected it.	
	30/7		Continued increasing accommodation of Camp by erecting marquees + necessary use of latrines.	
	1/8/16	9 am	Rev Mitchell proceeded on leave.	
	2/8/16	3 pm	Attended A.D.M.S Conference.	
	3/8/16	12 noon	Brigadier P. Officers Rest Station	
		2.30 p	Pay Out P. Officers Rest Station	
	3/8/16	6 pm	Visited Officers Rest Station	
	4/5/16	4 pm	Capt Patrick proceeded on 9 days Leave to Britain	
		9 am	Capt. O'Neill detailed to proceed on Brigade day with 107th Bde.	
	5/8/16	6 pm	Cinematograph Exhibition (two hours) given in the Barn to patients & Personnel	
			Through kindness of Major Peacock 9th Inniskillings.	
	6/8/16	10.45 a	A.D.M.S 36th Div: inspected the Camp & asked that his high appreciation of the good work done by the unit should be conveyed to all Officers NCOs + men concerned & said it reflected the greatest credit on all & was a source of great personal satisfaction to him.	

WAR DIARY
or
INTELLIGENCE SUMMARY.
(Erase heading not required.)

Army Form C. 2118.

Place	Date	Hour	Summary of Events and Information	Remarks and references to Appendices
Kleefzype	6/5/16	6.30 pm	6 Officers & 115 other ranks of 9th Inniskillings (German Meader Cordoli) departed	
	7/5/16	6 pm	Visited Officers Rest Station	
	8/5/16	6.30 pm	Visited Officers Rest Station	
	9/5/16	noon	Departed on 8 days leave to Ireland	
	9/5/16	4 pm	Returned from leave & received orders to proceed to the mess. Met D.D.M.S. & Col. every evening the trip in my service & visited army Rest Stan. Capt Reeve Saw the Q.M. of HEATH & Officer & Officers Rest Station with Capt Reeve	
			of Army	
	10/5/16	9 am	Received notification that the C in C means to inspect CLAIRFAYE.	
		1 pm	Visited Officers Rest Station.	
	11/5/16	10.30 am	Orders arrived to meet the C in C should he come. The C.n.C. did not come - Accompanies Adjcey 6 Officers, Non Ams the Corps Commander & Colo accompanied by the Ege 56 Div. from a visit to the Non-Ams - Went over ward & inspecting.	
		4 pm	training the all in readiness.	

WAR DIARY
or
INTELLIGENCE SUMMARY.
(Erase heading not required.)

Army Form C. 2118.

Place	Date	Hour	Summary of Events and Information	Remarks and references to Appendices
LAIRFAYE	11.5.16	10 am	The Rev. MITCHELL returns from leave.	
	12.5.16	10.45	The G.O.C. 36th Div. made a formal inspect of the 110th F.A. & the unit lines. He inspected everybody in every & expressed himself highly pleased with all the turnout & everything in every form and transport movement. Grenades and the promenade a half holiday.	
	13/5/16	11 am	Lt. LAMDIE returns from U.K.O.R.	
		3 pm	Divisional service & and Lt. LAMDIE 67 return M.O. 10th F.A.D. on air tax.	
	14/5/16	4 pm	Afternoon divisional service.	
	15/5/16	9 am	Capt. PATRICK returns off leave.	
		6 pm	Visits offices Nunt. Staten.	
	16/5/16	3 pm	Attend conference at Adjutancy Officer.	
	17/5/16		Posting of Units.	
	18/5/16	4 pm	Brewers & Corpl Adams & Col Sir CLAIR Oliver and Cleric and looks over the clear phone	

WAR DIARY
or
INTELLIGENCE SUMMARY.
(Erase heading not required.)

Army Form C. 2118.

Place	Date	Hour	Summary of Events and Information	Remarks and references to Appendices
CLAIRFAYE	19/6	9 p.m	Col. EMERSON visits Officers.	
"	20/6	7 a.m	Lt. FORBES took on scene - Had interviews & the President of Commune for	
"	21/6	2.15		
"	22/6	3 pm	attend conference at Recoury Officier	
"	23/6	2 pm	for defensive deposition.	
"	24/6	2 pm	Reinforces orders & deposition to bin & Officers acting front to division.	
"	25/6	2 pm	Col. EMERSON, O'NEIL & 6 NCOs went up to the evening & was then moved forward. Arriving front & was sent to see the President	
"	26/6	11 am	Brigade court Officier met Com. & sent to see the President of Army	
"	27/6	11 am	learning & Co's proceed on visits & came to see down to water supplies -	
"	28/6	10 am	Platoons fires & visits the morning.	
"	29/6	3 pm	Attends conf. at Recoury Officier.	

WAR DIARY
or
INTELLIGENCE SUMMARY.

(Erase heading not required.)

Army Form C. 2118.

Place	Date	Hour	Summary of Events and Information	Remarks and references to Appendices
Blair Atyn	29/5	9b	Lt. FORBES units off leave	
"	30/5	8 am	Capt O'NEIL to proceed on leave	
"	31/5	9 am	Surg. Lieut. McPHERSON & Ya-sor BLACK came & inspired the new Station defences & Camp & ordering occupants had —	Batt Seen doctor Lt Col Nunn O.C. 110 = Pr. Aun e

CONFIDENTIAL

110 F. Amb
Vol 9
June

WAR DIARY
of
7th
110 Field Ambulance

From 1st June 1916   To 30 June 1916

COMMITTEE FOR THE
MEDICAL HISTORY OF THE WAR
Date 5 AUG. 1915

VOLUME IX

CONFIDENTIAL

WAR DIARY
or
INTELLIGENCE SUMMARY.

Place	Date	Hour	Summary of Events and Information	Remarks and references to Appendices
CLAIRFAYE	1/6	11 a.m.	Orders taken round the Bdins 49th Div and to rest station.	
"	2/6	6 pm	Pensacry tough and around Clairfaye yesterday.	
"	3/6	9 am	Cpl O'NEIL pencilled in came. Pay out.	
"	"	10 am	Reports of arrival in rt area 9/6 to ordin & despatches to and coming here, also rt Hq and to stones dept. Supplies not	
"	4/6	3 pm	they should be sent here tomorrow. Lt BURROWS proceeded to Rue ambufance train depot & B.R.D. Reached own Cpl BERRY.	
"	5/6	9 am	the cycle of petting in - fount of it was started doing- Sent Pte GORDON to a course of instruction at Armour Officer	
"	6/6	3 pm	attached Company in Armour Office	
"	7/6	5 pm	Nothing of interest except a large amount of patrols men being sent in & around the Divisional Cdr's HARIDRGE pass on visits here	
"	8/6	4 am	Lt LAMBIE proceeded on leave	
"	"	10 am	Visits Officer Rent France	

WAR DIARY
or
INTELLIGENCE SUMMARY

(Erase heading not required.)

Army Form C. 2118.

Place	Date	Hour	Summary of Events and Information	Remarks and references to Appendices
CHIRFAYE(?)	8/7/16	10.20	Sept 4: Army Commander paid a visit to the post held by Division and saw the prisoners.	
"	9/7/16	6 am	Yorks & Lancs went on a train trip into the Division	
		1 pm	Arrived from Field Amb.	
"	10/7/16	11.30 am	Pioneers & Cattle forts(?) advised to be about the morning	
		4 pm	Lt. CLIMIE arrived from Company HQ.	
"	11/7/16	2.15 pm	Climie parade	
"	12/7/16	9 am	determined of CLIMIE to visit M.O. & R.S.R.	
		3.30 pm	arrived conference at Brigade Office	
"	13/7/16	9 am	Lt. CLIMIE proceeded to 10th R/frs to receive M.O. presenting in Camp.	
"	14/7/16	6 pm	Attended funeral conference in Brigade offices – Division arrest Division.	
"	15/7/16	9 am	Lt. CLIMIE arrived from 10th R/frs – M.O. did not press on Camp	
		2 pm	was at MARTINSART to arrange about Training and Camps and Classes	
"			part in TIMBERNAC WOOD.	
		3 pm	Transferred 43 cases to 49: Amm. Post Camp.	
"	16/7/16	6 am	Col. O'NEILL & Lt. CLIMIE and 38 ORs of Camps began here at MARTINSART	

WAR DIARY
or
INTELLIGENCE SUMMARY.
(Erase heading not required.)

Army Form C. 2118.

Place	Date	Hour	Summary of Events and Information	Remarks and references to Appendices
CLAIRFAYE	16/6/16	—	to relieve the 109th F.A. in the R.A.P.s at MARTINSART & evacuating posts in THIEPVAL WOOD & in Rd. bend of USINCRE, NORTH of AUTHUILLE. Officers to view.	
~	17/6/16	—		
~	18/6/16	11 AM	Been up to MARTINSART to view — the A.D.S. located in one the evacuating posts in THIEPVAL WOOD. Bearers are being used and bring down back to one dressed on the way sections from [?] Crucifix post & thence to one the [?] post for the M.O. Anderson Car Park.	
	3 PM			
	6 PM	Quiet to H.R. & his Adjutant.	
~	19/6/16	3 PM	Artillery continue to harass Enemy Offensive	
	2 PM	Been up to MARTINSART A.D.S. Enemy's shells etc and in one of being shelling. Reports to Enemy during times over and assisted shell in SPEYSIDE St.	
~	20/6/16			
~	21/6		Platoons X Corps posts on [?] his [?] morning. Officers to view.	

WAR DIARY
or
INTELLIGENCE SUMMARY.
(Erase heading not required.)

Army Form C. 2118.

Place	Date	Hour	Summary of Events and Information	Remarks and references to Appendices
CLAIRFAYE	22/6	4 pm	D.M.S. 4th Army paid a visit to an the hospitals rcvg & treating being evacuated.	
"	23/6	3.30 pm	Pr. Gen. JABES X Corps H.Q. paid a visit to an ambulances	
"	24/6	9 am	Search made made re entraining & evacuating pts for surgery canulae, ears & eyes.	
		11 am	Visited A.D.S. at MARTINSART	
		5 pm	Sent to F.S. Depôt at ENGLEBELMAR – BOUZINCOURT Rd. P.36.4.9.9. Map Sh. 57DSE to bring lighting smoke	1/20,000
"	25/6	6 pm	Sent 3 Horse Ambulance Wagons to FOREVICC to return 6— 100 P.A. for bringing lighty wded cases to F.A. to have to L/45 wded evacuees to stret coming here from medger 25/26.	
"	26/6	6 am	Pr evacuees came in in [?]—	
		12 m	23 lighty wded cases in [?]	
		9 pm	23 lighty wded cases in since 12 noon. A composition cap between	
"	27/6	6 am	appearing from Rein Floods. 55— evacuees in wh 6— F.G. prisoners.	

WAR DIARY or INTELLIGENCE SUMMARY

Army Form C. 2118.

Place	Date	Hour	Summary of Events and Information	Remarks and references to Appendices
CLAIRFAYE	27/6/16	11 a.m.	Wire received from O.C. No 2 Casualty Clearing Station, asking for our personnel to be sent across there - same wire to General for information.	
"	"	2 p.m.	Orders received from Armies to send O.C. & Adv. Party forward and instructed Lt PURCE & Lt 3 C. Pnt. to help with the transport & Wt. consisted.	
"	"	4 p.m.	Transport received for Advance party & Lt 3 Cs officers.	
"	"	6 p.m.	Received message from Lt PURCE that he had reached Lt CLIMIE at his posts, & Lt CLIMIE and me his wire came over of N° 3 C.P. for instructions - wired an early morning on duty to set men being made ready & might arrive to stop. Ordered to consult O.C.C.S. by train about 6 from 1/Bty. Also men ordered to ACHEUX Railway Stn. w/c to march to await a train at once sent by Hem. Ambulance.	
"	28/7/16	10 a.m.	R. Brown. Stretcher bearers under Cpl GRIMSON left 1/By with ambulance to L.G. PAISLEY AVENUE from No 2 C. Pnt.	
"	"	2 p.m.	2 Evans, 1 cor march & 1 cook non posted Reserve Coxns. Gang from wounded cases in 1/Bty.	

1577 Wt. W10791/1773 500,000 1/15 D. D. & L. A.D.S.S./Forms/C. 2118.

Place	Date	Hour	Summary of Events and Information	Remarks and references to Appendices
CLAIRFAYE	28/6/16	3 pm	Three men reported sick and sent to rendezvous at FORCEVILLE.	
		7 pm	Three men reported sick this evening. Two sick & another dying. M.A.C. Car sick, sent to hospital, stretcher and the prisoners to repatriate front line further orders —	
"	29/6/16	6 am	Seven wounded arrived during the night.	
		11.15am	Six men reported sick and were ordered to entrain to evacuate to C.C.S.	
		3 pm	Sent 5.9 cm. —	
		5 pm	Col. Atkinson's 2 men reported wounded. Relief sent up to replace them.	
"	30/6/16	8 am	21 wounded arrived during the night — lost 43 in at present.	
		3 pm	Drove X Corps water to dump here.	
		4 pm	Received 59 cars by field orders.	
		6 pm	S. G. Thompson AMS, pro — visit this evening.	
		7.30 pm	Sent Motor Cycle to report to 6½ N½ & Clearing Post at AVELUY wood for duty.	
		8.30 pm	Ave remaining motor ambulance cars sent to rendezvous at FORCEVILLE. Capt N.C. PATRICK proceeds to M.A.C. Car Pk Between DRUMON & Q'i Cr Road Je Q 10 2½ Aube —	

1 July 16
1 – 86 July
110 7 amb
Confidential

WAR DIARY
OF
110" FIELD AMBULANCE, R.A.M.C.

110 7 amb Vol 10

FROM 1ST JULY 1916   TO JULY 31ST 1916

VOLUME X

A.F. C 2118.

COMMITTEE FOR THE
MEDICAL HISTORY OF THE WAR
Date 5 - SEP 1915

WAR DIARY
or
INTELLIGENCE SUMMARY

(Erase heading not required.)

Army Form C. 2118

Place	Date	Hour	Summary of Events and Information	Remarks and references to Appendices
CLAIRFAYE	7/2/16	9 a.m.	Enemy a back to start 40 involved by train. Large numbers of wounded pass'd armies & came to see by train. 6 captures even large numbers.	
		11 a.m.	Loud shell arrives to Mont Renan, heavy bombardment & all sort of enemy army —	
		10 h.	Loud shell arrives on day. Green car on front 18 m in. art. Batty an actin coming to. Enemies by trail to be been very heavy loss of by loss very even 6 pm off. a few hunts.	
		2 a.m.	Enemy even very bad 6 pm though the morning etc. 60 wounded arrive coming in.	
		10 a.m.	Batteries firing & even & not to en't 65 wounded more & by	
	8/2/16		Some off'n hrs. fire 15 opn: Ren'n very acur's 6 clem en w of S Jn	
		12 n.	Late arriv'l. Total 375 wounded	
		5 h.	Mont Renan arrives & not.	
			Returns from out.	
		5 h.	Gen. Br. A.C. came in from RegtT & cleared about Tin	
		3 h.	Enemy active 6 add 6 m of Renan.	
		11 l.	Have even many about 1.0 m.	

Army Form C. 2118

WAR DIARY
or
INTELLIGENCE SUMMARY
(Erase heading not required.)

Place	Date	Hour	Summary of Events and Information	Remarks and references to Appendices
PLAINFAYE	2/3/16	10 a.m.	Carried out anti-aircraft practice between hours 10 a.m. to 12 noon	
		12 n.	Lt. D.G. Abud & Lt. ARTHUR SLIGGETT and experienced men sent down.	
	3/4/16	10 h.	Have now only about 12 guns left.	
		10 a.m.	Orders received to my that the Division is being withdrawn from the line & I am to proceed with the 5 the Cont. Asty. B.G. & 10 I am to remain in CLAIRFAYE for the present.	
	3/5/16	5 h.	Lent to an O.C. of incoming unit.	
		11 a.m.	Handed over 6·½·, 6·in Asty, Brit. Ambulance & 36·pdr. Brit. of 109·R.A. & also Officers	
		1 h.	and NCO's. Orders received to be ready to move at 6 p.m.	
		3 h.	Mess-packs & all ranks & evacuated the appartment &	
		5 h.	Capt. & Adjutant to the mess.	
		6 p.m.	Hence marched to SEPTEMBRE at 6 hour.	
			Started for SEPTEMBRE via LEALVILLERS, TOUTENCOURT, HERISSART - RUBEMPRÉ.	

WAR DIARY
or
INTELLIGENCE SUMMARY

(Erase heading not required.)

Army Form C. 2118

Instructions regarding War Diaries and Intelligence Summaries are contained in F.S. Regs., Part II. and the Staff Manual respectively. Title Pages will be prepared in manuscript.

Place	Date	Hour	Summary of Events and Information	Remarks and references to Appendices
SEPTENVILLE	5/7/16	9.30h	Arrived at SEPTENVILLE & for men in huts & Officers to the byres.	
"	6/7/16	10 am	Sent the men to work & repair the loopen & the ready to move at any time.	
		6 pm	Had orders to had hrs audience to proceed on a moment's notice to any place they may be detailed to be in readiness to move at ½ hr. notice from 6 am tomorrow.	
"	7/7/16	10.30 am	Orders came thro' and we moved to the Field Ambulance. All waters proceed to his Officers.	
"	8/7/16	6 pm	No news to report my any to answer in his Officers.	
"	9/7/16	—	Still at SEPTONVILLE. Awaiting to move	
"		10 am	Orders paid a visit — to Lt. J. Aulemore	
"		12 m	Capt. W. S. BERRY. Name reported for duty	
"	10/7/16	6.15 am	Left SEPTONVILLE & marched to BEAUVAL	
BEAUVAL	"	1 pm	Arrived BEAUVAL & went into Billet.	
"	11/7/16	6.15 am	Left BEAUVAL via CANDAS & marched to PROUVILLE.	
PROUVILLE	"	10.15 am	Arrived PROUVILLE & went into Billet.	

WAR DIARY
or
INTELLIGENCE SUMMARY
(Erase heading not required.)

Army Form C. 2118

Instructions regarding War Diaries and Intelligence Summaries are contained in F.S. Regs., Part II. and the Staff Manual respectively. Title Pages will be prepared in manuscript.

Place	Date	Hour	Summary of Events and Information	Remarks and references to Appendices
PROUVILLE	12/6	1.30 am	8 Lt. PROUVILLE & went to CONTEVILLE.	
CONTEVILLE	"	2.30 am	Arrived CONTEVILLE	
		3.6 am	Staff & return.	
		6. am	Left CONTEVILLE by Car to BERGUETTE.	
BERGUETTE	"	10. am	Arrived and returned	
		12 m	Staff & went to CAMPAGNE	
		6 pm	Arrived and went into Billet.	
CAMPAGNE	" 13/6	1.30 pm	Left CAMPAGNE & went to WESTROVE	
		6.30 pm	Arrived and billets to the major in CHATEAU de VERGUETTE and to be near to 10 & 2 Corps.	
WESTROVE	14/6	10 am	Assume command to an went around to lines.	
		10.30 am	Lunch with Army & find that the return to lines did not anything & do we send the 1st to be based & find [...] out return - Germans seem - interior points & find 10th & R. [...]	
	15/6	2 pm	10 & 2. A Patrols active & frank prominence and team	
		10 am	Capt. W. S. HAY left & report & returns to hosp on croix H.Q.	
		11 am	B.G. 107 Reco- going - various.	
		2 pm	Meet in march of the R.A. head.	

WAR DIARY
or
INTELLIGENCE SUMMARY
(Erase heading not required.)

Army Form C. 2118

Instructions regarding War Diaries and Intelligence Summaries are contained in F. S. Regs., Part II. and the Staff Manual respectively. Title Pages will be prepared in manuscript.

Place	Date	Hour	Summary of Events and Information	Remarks and references to Appendices
WESTROVE	16/7/16	2 pm	Lieut. Gen. Porter - D.M.S. 2nd Army visited F.A. 1 Sect.	
	17/7/16	2 pm	Sanitary Officer 2nd Army inspected the camp & vicinity.	
	18/7/16	10 am	Horse & kit inspection of the unit.	
		2 pm	Route march.	
	19/7/16	4 pm	Officers & orderlies formed a wind & went out round the camp.	
		6 pm	Men received to kits my arm in readiness to move.	
		11 pm	Orders received to march at 10 am to BOLZEELE Area.	
	20/7/16	10 am	Left WESTROVE to BOLZEELE. I went in advance to ascertain where we. Met hiring offr. on the way from me that I should have rue to WATTEN. & the message have would have. I am informed that my unit has gone to A. & VOLKRINCKHOVE.	
VOLKRINCKHOVE	21/7/16	4 pm	Left VOLKRINCKHOVE to WORMHOUTE. Sent leaving party.	
		6.30 am	Arrived in WORMHOUTE - Buses Mr. of the injun.	
WORMHOUTE		4 pm	Orders received to move at 8.30 am.	
	22/7/16	8.30 am	Left WORMHOUTE to HOLENDEN Area.	
		4 pm	Arrived at LE BREARDE & made to bivin.	
LE BREARDE		6 pm	Orders received to march to BAILLEUL next morning & await ambulances	

WAR DIARY
or
INTELLIGENCE SUMMARY
(Erase heading not required.)

Army Form C. 2118

Place	Date	Hour	Summary of Events and Information	Remarks and references to Appendices
La BREARDE	23/7/16	5.30 am	Party to take over from 61st F.A. at 16 RUE DE METEREN - BAILLEUL.	
		10 am	Advance party (O. Emerson) left. Capt. PURCE left on motorcycle. Lieuts — Sisters and C. NEARY to obtain Cars.	
			CORKLEY proceeding on leave.	
			Left w/c arrived to F.A. at BAILLEUL.	
	24/7/16	1 pm	Arrived & joined Hdqrs of 61st F.A. but took over any orders to remain near Division.	
		5 pm	Took over from 61st F.A. Orderly room, received any instructions and others up duties & arrived unit of 1st & 107 Field.	
		10 am	Staff sent to arrange 1st places, prepare to receive sick. C. Baker opened up.	
	25/7/16	9 pm	Wounded & sick arrived to be evacuated to Base. No intimation for arrangements to be made to the Back to NEUVE EGLISE.	
		10 am	Received by Divisional orders to run the trek & we were instructed to run these. — Several importance support.	
		4 pm	Arrived, D.&R.M.S. fm -- with us to the 2nd Australian.	
	26/7/16	10 am	Capt. MOIR went to relieve M.O. at 16 A.S.R. proceeding in same Paid a visit to the Baths.	
	27/7/16	5 pm	Nothing to note.	
	28/7/16	—	—	
	29/7/16	10 am	D. D. M. S. & Gen'l Cator inspected the Field Ambulance & time Service.	

Army Form C. 2118

WAR DIARY
or
INTELLIGENCE SUMMARY
(Erase heading not required.)

Place	Date	Hour	Summary of Events and Information	Remarks and references to Appendices
BAILLEUL	20/6	11 am	Orders & Paris & Laird & un finest. The idea forever we entering the heavy rain.	
"	31/6	—	going 15 mi—	

B.H. Sven Brown
Lt Col Neuve
gc 110th Fd. Anne

B.E.F.

SUMMARY OF MEDICAL WAR DIARIES OF 110th F.A. 36th Div.

8th Corps. 5th ARMY.

19th Corps from 26th July.
4th Corps 3rd Army from 23rd August.

Western Front Operations - July-Aug. 1917.

Officer Commanding - Lt.Col. B.H.V. DUNBAR.
Officer Commanding - Major R.G. Meredith from 15th August.

SUMMARISED UNDER THE FOLLOWING HEADINGS:-

Phase "D" 1. - Passchendaele Operations -"July-Nov.1917."
(a) - Operations commencing July 1917.

B.E.F.

1.

<u>110th F.A. 36th Div. 8th Corps.</u>   Western Front.
<u>5th ARMY.</u>   July 1917.
<u>Officer Commanding - Lt.Col. B.H.V.DUNBAR.</u>
<u>19th Corps from 26th July.</u>

<u>PHASE "D" 1. - Passchendaele Operations-"July-Nov. 1917"</u>

    (a) - <u>Operations commencing July 1917.</u>

<u>Headquarters at Renescure.</u>

July 7th.   Transferred from 2nd Army.

         <u>Moves.</u> To La Wattine.

8th.   <u>Decorations.</u> Pte. Donelly and McKay awarded M.M. for Operations 7th - 8th June.

    <u>Operations R.A.M.C.</u>) D.R.S. opened in tents.
    <u>Med. Arrangements.</u>)

17th.   <u>Decorations.</u> S.M. Bell awarded Médaille Militaire.

20th.   <u>Moves.</u>) To Esquerdes and opened up D.R.S.
    <u>Ops. R.A.M.C.</u>)

25th.   <u>Moves.</u> To Setque for Winnizeele.

26th.   <u>Transfer.</u> To 19th Corps.

B.E.F.

110th F.A.   36th Div.   19th Corps.   Western Front.
                                            July-Aug. 1917.
5th ARMY.

Officer Commanding - Lt.Col.B.H.V.DUNBAR.

Major R.G. MEREDITH to O.C. from 15th August.

PHASE "D"   1. - Passchendaele Operations - "July-Nov.1917"

(a) - Operations commencing July 1917.

Headquarters at Oudezeele.

July 26th.   Transfer.   To 19th Corps.

              Moves.   To Oudezeele.

    27th.   Moves.   Detachment.   2 & 19 to 64th C.C.S.

    30th.   2 & 41 to C.W.W.S. Vlamertinghe Mill.

              Moves.   To Watou area K.24.c.9.8.

    31st.   Moves Detachment.   1 and B.S.D. and 5 M. Ambulances

              to Red Farm.

                                    Returned 3/8.

B.E.F.

1.

<u>110th F.A. 36th Div. 8th Corps.</u>   Western Front.
　　　　　　　　　　　　　　　　　　　　July 1917.
<u>5th ARMY.</u>

Officer Commanding - Lt.Col. E.T.V.DUNBAR.

<u>19th Corps from 26th July.</u>

<u>PHASE "D" 1. - Passchendaele Operations-"July-Nov. 1917"</u>

　　(a) - <u>Operations commencing July 1917.</u>

<u>Headquarters at Renescure.</u>

July 7th.　Transferred from 2nd Army.

　　　　　<u>Moves.</u> To La Wattine.

　8th.　<u>Decorations.</u> Pte. Donelly and McKay awarded M.M. for Operations 7th - 8th June.

　　　　<u>Operations R.A.M.C.</u>) D.R.S. opened in tents.
　　　　<u>Med. Arrangements.</u>)

　17th.　<u>Decorations.</u> S.M. Bell awarded Medaille Militaire.

　20th.　<u>Moves.</u>   ) To Esquerdes and opened up D.R.S.
　　　　<u>Ops. R.A.M.C.</u>)

　25th.　<u>Moves.</u> To Setque for Winnizeele.

　26th.　<u>Transfer.</u> To 19th Corps.

B.E.F.

110th F.A. 36th Div. 19th Corps.   Western Front.
                                            July-Aug. 1917.
5th ARMY.

Officer Commanding - Lt.Col.B.R.V.DUNBAR.

Major R.G. MEREDITH to O.C. from 15th August.

PHASE "D" 1. - Passchendaele Operations - "July-Nov.1917"

    (a) - Operations commencing July 1917.

Headquarters at Oudezeele.

July 26th.   Transfer.   To 19th Corps.
             Moves. To Oudezeele.
     27th.   Moves. Detachment. 2 & 19 to 64th C.C.S.
     30th.   2 & 41 to C.W.W.S. Vlamertinghe Mill
             Moves. To Watau area K..24.c.9.S.
     31st.   Moves Detachment.   1 and B.S.D. and 5 M. Ambulances
             to Red Farm.
                                    Returned 3/8.

August 1916
36th (Ulster) Div.

WAR DIARY

of

110th FIELD AMBULANCE R.A.M.C.

From August 1st 1916 to August 31st 1916

VOLUME XI

August 31st 1916

COMMITTEE FOR THE
MEDICAL HISTORY OF THE WAR
Date -9 OCT. 1916

Army Form C. 2118

WAR DIARY
or
INTELLIGENCE SUMMARY
(Erase heading not required.)

Instructions regarding War Diaries and Intelligence Summaries are contained in F.S. Regs., Part II. and the Staff Manual respectively. Title Pages will be prepared in manuscript.

Place	Date	Hour	Summary of Events and Information	Remarks and references to Appendices
BAILLEUL	1/6	—	Nothing to note.	
"	2/6	2 pm	Paid over the troops.	
"	3/6	10 am	Detailed Col. EMERSON & O'NEIL to proceed to A.D.S. & 10th & 11th F.A.	
			& see the evacuation of wounded from the front line.	
			Visit from Army.	
"	4/6	5 pm	Major Col. COMYN-ARMS on his farewell. Desired to meet all	
		10.30 am	of the Officers.	
		11 am	Attended Brigade Church on Sunday with Col. EMERSON &	
			examined P.B. men – the Arrival in mountains.	
		2 pm	Noticed from Brigade.	
		3 pm	Visit received to detail Col. W.S. BERRY to report on Officers	
			& depart to Corps to see in charging in the absence of Mr. IMMIE	
		6 pm	Col. BERRY reports on Officers & Drawing to Corps.	
"	5/6	8.1 pm	Officers men never on the evacuation of his wound by 15th & 16th Div.	
			men & A.D.S. 1 Ncb & 6 O.R. & KHANDAHR FARM on 1 hr	
		9 pm	Seven 1 Ncb & 6 O.R. & DRANOUTRE by 11 am normal.	
	6/6	10 am	Capt. O'NEIL & 10 O.R. reports to Hos. over A.D.S. & DRANOUTRE	

WAR DIARY
or
INTELLIGENCE SUMMARY
(Erase heading not required.)

Army Form C. 2118

Instructions regarding War Diaries and Intelligence Summaries are contained in F. S. Regs., Part II. and the Staff Manual respectively. Title Pages will be prepared in manuscript.

Place	Date	Hour	Summary of Events and Information	Remarks and references to Appendices
BAILLEUL	6/6	12 m	Message received from C.O. O/N.E/L reporting having taken over duties at DRANOUTRE & requesting A.D.S. the please be made ready	
		3.20 pm	for clearing and reporting to them to take up work the same.	
		4 pm	Cpl PURCE received H. even:	
		7/6 11. am	Paid = visit to A.D.S. DRANOUTRE & 1/2 Dover/Tg Offr	
		6.15 pm	Visited Bond. Both.	
		12 —		
		3 pm	Accompanied It. Arring to A.D.S.	
		5 pm	Nature received to detain Cpl PURCE & note to Brid Sanitary	
		10 pm	Officer — this received to detain M.O to relieve M.O 16 N.I.R – end.	
			Cpl BERRY received from dept to V Corps —	
			Orders Cpl BERRY to relieve M.O 16 N.I.N. the 16 N.I.R came	
	8/6	6 am	in to food – Cpl BERRY nails here –	
		9 am	Reports that to Brens.	
		10 am	Cpl PURCE reports to buy, M/C Ind. Sanitary Offr –	
		11 am	Suns evening party to Brend, composed of 2nd M.O.	
			brids received on reture of 16 N.I.N. Cpl BERRY proceeds	
			to to Reserve.	

WAR DIARY or INTELLIGENCE SUMMARY

Army Form C. 2118

(Erase heading not required.)

Instructions regarding War Diaries and Intelligence Summaries are contained in F. S. Regs., Part II. and the Staff Manual respectively. Title Pages will be prepared in manuscript.

Place	Date	Hour	Summary of Events and Information	Remarks and references to Appendices
BAILLEUL	9/7/16	2 pm	Paid a visit to A.D.S. found work going on well.	
"	10/7/16	6/am	Capt BERRY arrived for temporary duty vice 16 N.I.R.	
"	11/7/16	10 am	Arrived inspect. No. D.S. lines and round the front.	
"	"	2.30 pm	Could, for events & went to A.D.S. & are about relieving – phone to Bng N.J. Arrived & found any well. There please.	
"	12/7/16	10 am	Lieut arrived from Bedard as temporary relief. R.A.P.S. on 107 Ads from Recum point Ardres to HAZEBROUCK	
"	13/7/16	2.30 5 pm	Paid a visit to the Butts and also to the A.D.S. at DRANOUTRE	
"	14/7/16	12. m	Went to KHANDAHAR FARM from m to ST. QUENTIN CABARET & PONT DE ST QUENTIN to meet O.C 121 Inf. Regt. But – met G – making some there front there.	
"	"	6/pm	Reported to asserve visit on invet. Capt MOIR arrived from 12 C.C.S	
"	15/7/16	2 pm	Sent Capt HAY to D-12 C.C.S HAZEBROUCK	
"	16/7/16	4/pm	Capt MOIR down to A.D.S. for duty. Capt BERRY to Beoten during chance of Car – HAY.	
"	17/7/16	3 pm	Paid a visit to the Butts. Situation is not improving are taking	
"	18/7/16	11 am	Cases to hostile & went to A.D.S. all being.	

WAR DIARY
or
INTELLIGENCE SUMMARY
(Erase heading not required.)

Army Form C. 2118

Place	Date	Hour	Summary of Events and Information	Remarks and references to Appendices
BAILLEUL	19/5/16	—	Nothing to note	
"	20/5/16	3pm	Distribution of 6mm x 1 St. Cyr. The ambulance being on 1 hour's house party	
"	21/5/16	5 E. C. G.	6 mm to Pont to help R.E. N.Z. at the work	
		10am	Sent 20 men to repair S-Q QUENTIN CABARET to meters	
		4pm	2 stores parties taking note to R.A. P's.	
"	22/5/16	4pm	A/Lieuty. first — visit — inspected site to prepare huts standings	
		6 p.m.	Capt RUSSELL moved to new permanent and Taken on the strength.	
			Reported amount to General.	
"	23/5/16	10 am	O.C. RUSSELL w/P.M.T. and his son from APM 9th Corps - He is to dropped Berlin to await news re it to into the evening. The news is & ordinary expectation. Reported to APM 9th Corps. Was received	
			From 107 R&R convening this man.	
"	24/5/16	2pm	Went to OMS to hear the orders & arrears, but they did not arrive	
			Found an envelope. Party on to home.	
"	25/5/16	10am	Sent officer to Depot Cave to inspect site for hut standings. Me	
"	26/5/16	4pm	An officer from the Corps came to inspect site for hut standings. He and would left site. & proper must arise down to the permanent one.	
"	27/5/16	10am	Q.T. & Q.M. HEATH proceeded on 7 days leave today.	
		12 m.	Cpl. HAY received from N/12 C.C.S. HAZEBROUCK.	

WAR DIARY
or
INTELLIGENCE SUMMARY

(Erase heading not required.)

Army Form C. 2118

Instructions regarding War Diaries and Intelligence Summaries are contained in F.S. Regs., Part II. and the Staff Manual respectively. Title Pages will be prepared in manuscript.

Place	Date	Hour	Summary of Events and Information	Remarks and references to Appendices
BAILLEUL	28/16	3pm	Orders issued this afternoon & on this & two fine & two new letters were received.	
"	29/16	11 am	Orders came too & two men received intimation.	
		2.30	Paid visit to Pts, APDS to DRANOUTRE, HAY R.M.G. crud.	
		5 pm	Lieut Capt BERRY & Read KANDAHAR FARM not seen above.	
	30/16	2 am	Capt BERRY returned to HQ.	
"	31/16	3pm	Capt MOIR proceeded to OXELEAR for a short course on the anti-gas ochre.	
				B.H seen Bapten L.t. Clemme hunn Nr 11.15 & annr

36th Div

WAR DIARY

110 7th FIELD AMBULANCE

CONFIDENTIAL
Sept. 1916

from Sept 1st 1916 to Sept 30th 1916

VOLUME XII

COMMITTEE FOR THE
MEDICAL HISTORY OF THE WAR
Date 30 OCT 1915

C2118.
30 9/16

WAR DIARY
or
INTELLIGENCE SUMMARY
(Erase heading not required.)

Army Form C. 2118

Instructions regarding War Diaries and Intelligence Summaries are contained in F.S. Regs., Part II. and the Staff Manual respectively. Title Pages will be prepared in manuscript.

Place	Date	Hour	Summary of Events and Information	Remarks and references to Appendices
BAILLEUL	1/7	3½pm	Rec'd instruction to send our ambulance car to 105 R.A. to help the evacuation of wounded. This Car on return used as sect. car of the MO. of the evacuated	
"	2/6	10 am	section. Cpl Rosseau to relieve M.O. 9th R.I.R. who is taken sick	
"	3/6	10.30 am	pronounced sick. A.R., R.M.S., and Officers came to see how the train line - frying worked on and the work is to settle immediately. Cpl. MOIR relieved from Bailleul, proceed & proceed join & 2005	
		3 pm	DRANOUTRE.	
"	4/6	5 pm	Sent extra men as reinforcement to re-arranging of the ads. of the horse of J. as unwell by the	
"	5/6	10 am	1st A.D.S. at DRANOUTRE & the 109 = R.A. Handed our 1st A.D.S. at DRANOUTRE	
"	6/6	1 pm	Reinforcements received from DRANOUTRE	
		10 am	Sent 1 officer & 14 N.Co's men to ADS TROIS ROIS to take over from the 10th R.A. Car, 1 officer & 10 men to KHANDAHAR	
"		6 pm	FARM to take over the ambulance post there Reports to arriving 105 reliefs has been carried out & having taken over from the 105 R.A.	

WAR DIARY
or
INTELLIGENCE SUMMARY

(Erase heading not required.)

Army Form C. 2118

Place	Date	Hour	Summary of Events and Information	Remarks and references to Appendices
BAILLEUL	9/16	10 am	Went to visit the A.D.S. & see everything just there on from the 1st F.A. Found all in order. A large amount of work to do, the men & nos. of casualties. But we set to & organised things & in a way of carrying on. Received nothing to signify to officers & men of strong & being to men of return & troops & our Received reports etc. Received from Arras.	
		2 pm	Sent two Ambulance cars to Arras to move some men arriving	
		5.30 pm	from HAZEBROUCK, being brought to the rails & being to vehicles	
		11.45 pm	Began arrival from Arras.	
	9/16	5 pm	Attempts made to send Co= PURCE & visit M. O.É & M.M.	
		—	proceeding on route.	
	9/16	10 am	On empty arrival to O.C. KHANDAHAR FARM & back & being in 2 mile Ambulance waiting to return.	
		12 m	Motor Ambulance came. They are handed out by a Steam & Colley	
			Convoy.	
		1.30 pm	Went to Arras & TROIS ROIS & Arras. BMG.	
		3 pm	Arrived at Army Office.	
	12/16	10 am / 1 pm	Accompanied by Asst Director Medical Service in evacuating post Peline	

WAR DIARY
or
INTELLIGENCE SUMMARY.
(Erase heading not required.)

Army Form C. 2118.

Place	Date	Hour	Summary of Events and Information	Remarks and references to Appendices
BAILLEUL	13/6/16	11 am	Capt. HENNESSY arrived from leave & posted to 15th units. He is vice Lt RUSSELL	
"	14/6/16	10.30 am	Orders were an improve to the horse lines during First & Second line transport	
"	15/6/16	10 am	went to Trois Rois 87 & Advance Camps to see 1st R.E. re posting important to Khandahar farm	
"	16/6/16	—	Capt. HENNESSY L-P to 6th 15th D.A.C. vice M.O. going on leave. Acting L-P unit	
"	17/6/16	10 am	Went to KHANDAHAR FARM & TROIS ROIS. All work going on satisfactorily.	
"	18/6/16	10 am	Taken over the Chateau in MONT NOIR & advised re Stables an offices	
			Rode to the TX Sectn. Capt EMERSON returns to a O.E.	
		3 pm	Orders issued to 8.A. horse lines and transport	
"	19/6/16	11 am	Went to MONT NOIR to arrange about the Officers Quarters	
	20/6/16	10 am	went to KHANDAHAR FARM & TROIS ROIS & the Batt. All work going	
	21/6/16	5 pm	went to MONT NOIR vice Ordering	
	22/6/16	5 pm	350 men of the 11th Lincolnshire Regt came to Lines at 1 am & let for G.R.	

WAR DIARY
or
INTELLIGENCE SUMMARY

(Erase heading not required.)

Army Form C. 2118

Place	Date	Hour	Summary of Events and Information	Remarks and references to Appendices
BAILLEUL	23/9/16	10 am	Capt HAY to be M.O. of Trois Rois in addition to training the Bath & Capt BERRY the present to MONT NOIR to take charge of Officer Men other ranks Capt EMERSON proceeds to no troops ranks	
		11 am	1 NCO's & men to active service to battalion & medical officers were sent as experts in Officers NCO's & men of the Division.	
	24/9/16	7.30 am	Capt EMERSON proceed on 14 days leave.	
		10 am	Capt HENNESY received from training troop & proceeds to ATHOLSBURG	
		3 pm	FARM to relieve Capt O'HIGG.	
			Capt O'NEIL relieved Lt. Liewen & proceeds to "Red Bar" to review	
	25/9/16	—	M.O. proceeding on leave. training in use	
	26/9/16	10 am	Been told by escort went about during trials & inspecting out. an	
			Reference is made	
		4 pm	Visit Officer home post on MONT NOIR	
	27/10	11 am	Orders respect will Carrying stations	
		4 pm	assisted hither and dispense Officer to examine Officers he Common Communication	
	28/9/16	—	Nothing from.	

WAR DIARY
or
INTELLIGENCE SUMMARY

(Erase heading not required.)

Army Form C. 2118

Place	Date	Hour	Summary of Events and Information	Remarks and references to Appendices
BAILLEUL	29/6	10 am	Paid a visit to Officers now billeted in Mont Noir. All going satisfactorily. Lunched and from in the care of the Somme Farm estaminet.	
"	30/6	2 pm		

B.H. Jean Barton
Lt Col comdt
O/c 11th D. Amb

140/1815.

36/1213.

Oct. 1916

110th Field Ambulance.

COMMITTEE FOR THE
MEDICAL HISTORY OF THE WAR
Date −9 DEC. 1916

Vol 13

Army Form C. 2118

WAR DIARY or INTELLIGENCE SUMMARY

110th Field Ambulance

(Erase heading not required.)

Place	Date	Hour	Summary of Events and Information	Remarks and references to Appendices
BAILLEUL	1/10	—	Nothing to note	
"	3/10	—	Proceeded on 10 days leave to England. Handed over to Capt. McPatrick BMO Senior Officer present	
"	4/10	9 am	Taken over temporary command of F.A.	
"	"	3 pm	190 men 15 N.C.O. & divisional Band came here to be paid. Pay ok.	
"	5/10	10 am	Capt O'NEIL visits — Handed over from ? Trou Rois	
"	"	3 pm	Capt MOIR visits. Handed over from ? Trou Rois in ? ——	
"			received out to 15 bay.	
"		4.30 noon	14 = N.S.N came here to be —— Received proposal.	
"	6/10	11 am	Capt O'NEIL reported his return from 7= Return Battalion to his	
"	8/10	10 am	Capt MOIR proceeded — 10 days leave to —— & Marseilles.	
"	9/10	4.30 noon	6 = N.S.N. + 100 men 16 = N.S.N came here to be ——	
"	10/10	11 am	Argent in —— hospital & transport ——	
"	12/10	3 pm	Capt EMERSON reported his arrival from ——	
"		4	10 = N.S.N & Field Band to be	

WAR DIARY
or
INTELLIGENCE SUMMARY
(Erase heading not required.)

Army Form C. 2118

Place	Date	Hour	Summary of Events and Information	Remarks and references to Appendices
BAILLEUL	12/10	3pm	Capt BERRY rejoined from Mont Noir, handed instructions from Bthms	
"	14/10	11am	Capt EMERSON went up to relieve him. Lt Col DUNBAR returned from leave.	Lt P Paßruh Cpt-leave
"	15/10	—	Returned from leave & resumed command of R.A.	
"	15/10	11.30 am	Church parade.	
"		4pm	Various officers Nor Pfaci at HONT NOIR	
"	16/10	9.30 am	Lunch G Division. Detn. G.O.C. 36 Dir inspect Fd Ambs.	
"		11 am	Lunch G ADMS at TROIS ROIS.	
"	17/10	10 am	Lunch G 101 Bde H.Q. & gun back to Antoine Road in a new motor ambe reported. Cpt PERRY proceeded on 14 days leave.	
"	18/10	10 am	Quentin's Lt Ravid G KHANDAHAR FARM. Posts & The Rye Aid Post.	
"			Remained Jannin Murray to Entre G P.G.C.M.	
"	19/10	11am	Agenda inspect Mars Draving Ptms, Guides & horse lines	
"		4.30 pm	From 107 Bde came to tea.	

WAR DIARY or INTELLIGENCE SUMMARY

(Erase heading not required.)

Army Form C. 2118

Place	Date	Hour	Summary of Events and Information	Remarks and references to Appendices
BAILLEUL	20/2/16	10 am	Inspn: Offrs' Mess First Aid Mont Noir – Behind IX Corps horse amb. inspection.	
	21/2/16	10.30 am	Aerodrome Abeele C= Rest Trois Rois. Visits Murray hrs by L.G.C.M. Services suspended.	
	22/2/16	12 nn	Rennepts service & Aux- Marie – Sp. JARRETT & Pte FITZGERALD awarded to a Military Medal. L Forward Ambulance to Rest & Corps Commander 9: Area inspected from Mon.	
		3 p	Capt MOIR recce rft of Front.	
	23/2/16	5 am	Capt O'NEIL proceed on 10 days contact course.	
		12 nn	Advance party to Ribbon to Divisional Hosts – 10 preds hrs. C ——— NCO's men 107, 109 + 115. F.a.	
	24/2/16	4.30	NCO's men 10+ B-ce Amsts hrs L Ton.	
	25/2/16	10 am	Aerodrome to Reims & Klondike Farm & Skirmishing from C nnn in Mon N.A.P. are each party on ready. S.M. BAKER founded on "L.Dep" Course	
	26/2/16	9 am		
	27/2/16	3 pm	Mem of 14 = A.M. enemt men for Ton –	

WAR DIARY
or
INTELLIGENCE SUMMARY
(Erase heading not required.)

Army Form C. 2118

Instructions regarding War Diaries and Intelligence Summaries are contained in F. S. Regs., Part II. and the Staff Manual respectively. Title Pages will be prepared in manuscript.

Place	Date	Hour	Summary of Events and Information	Remarks and references to Appendices
Brimeux	28/6	3pm	Leave to Trois Rois. AOS to airport.	
	29/6	—	Nothing to report	
	29/6	3pm	Leave to Officers Mess Stores - Brass keys trim	
	30/6	10 am	OC Divis eye today for N-2.5 CCS on Europe by water stay	
			2nd Army.	
	31/6	10 am	Aeroplanes arrive to KHANDAHAR FARM & TROIS ROIS	
		3p	Arrows inform 14 Q & P.A. > have trains in	
		4.30	Divis 2nd Army inspect 14 Q & 15 P. Aviseau.	
			Court to 107th Rifle Corner to Sen.	
			B.H. Jean Braun	
			Lt. Col Nante	
			9c 110th Fd. Ambn	

36th Div.

110th Field Ambulance.

140/1262

Nov. 1916

COMMITTEE FOR THE
MEDICAL HISTORY OF THE WAR
Date -3 JAN.1917

WAR DIARY or INTELLIGENCE SUMMARY

Army Form C. 2118

110 Fd Amb

Vol 14

Place	Date	Hour	Summary of Events and Information	Remarks and references to Appendices
BAILLEUL	1/6	8 am	Capt. W. S. BERRY received from event. Corps up to Bailleul. Batt. & Capt. J. TROIS ROIS arrive at	
		10 am	Sanitary office. At time about 15 prisoners of the field.	
	2/6	4 p	Paid two visits to 1 N.Z. Genl Hosp.	
		3 p	Relieves 1 NCO & 10 men also sent to prevent a vacancy party	
			in the Batt. to a forward G.T. 109: Q.O. C. ran & m. coming	
			parts Hqrs.	
		10 am	Capt BERRY detains to make to meet M.O. ? 9: Refers	
		1.30	marching on 1st Supp event. Capt Berry & proceed 15 separ	
		p	forth and to pay all settlements on MONT NOIR, Bois, TROIS ROIS	
	3/6	3½ hr	& KHANDAMAR FARM.	
			Leave Q head Qrs to see some entries in forward a dressing n	
			visiting first post.	
		11.30	A party of 107 Polish camera G Ldn.	
	4/6	3 pm	Capt BERRY to the visits G M.O. from 109 F.A. & CO agent CO D.S.D.A.J	
			G put on a dressing avoir ask is never in event.	
	5/6	11 am	Capt BERRY	
	6/6	9.30	Capt BERRY visits from 9: R/en. in expect to any - on attained W Catn n - outgoing movement.	

WAR DIARY or INTELLIGENCE SUMMARY

Army Form C. 2118

Place	Date	Hour	Summary of Events and Information	Remarks and references to Appendices
BAILLEUL	6/7/16	10 am	Lecture C/O KHANDAHAR FARM - Cook worky finished.	
		12 n	" C/O TROIS ROIS & Loane Redt.	
		3 pm	Capt MOIR detailed to carry out reconnaissance of 107 M.G.C & T.M.B. billets & one	
	7/7/16		Artillery & one	
	8/7/16	6 am	L/. Q.M. HEATH proceeded on 10 days leave to Eng.	
		10 am	Capt. O'NEIL returned from leave.	
	9/7/16	7 pm	Capt. O'NEIL sworn to relieve Capt. CHRISTIE, the latter to —	
		11	report him for duty.	
	10/7/16	10 pm	Various — TROIS ROIS & Battn. Duties — KHAN DAHAR FARM - under the enemy gunfire. Enemy [?] on pilot railway line.	
	12/7/16	12 n	Armourers visited Officers Nos Steel on MONT NOIR	
	13/7/16	10 am	TROIS Division Rest and Dressing Post in Trois Rois	
	14/7/16	4.30 pm	A party of 129 RSR came to town.	
	15/7/16	3 pm	Paid a visit to Officers post at Mont Noir.	
	16/7/16	10 am	Inspected Khandahar Farm & Trois Rois Billets.	

WAR DIARY
or
INTELLIGENCE SUMMARY
(Erase heading not required.)

Army Form C. 2118

Instructions regarding War Diaries and Intelligence Summaries are contained in F.S. Regs, Part II. and the Staff Manual respectively. Title Pages will be prepared in manuscript.

Place	Date	Hour	Summary of Events and Information	Remarks and references to Appendices
BAILLEUL	16/6/16	3 pm	Orders imposed Main Dressing Station inspected.	
	15/6/16	8.30	Orders came here for - experiment of horse offices.	
		3 pm	Visits A.D.S. Trois Rois.	
	18/6/16	3 pm	Cpln BERRY returned fr. listening duty over Tr. Corps.	
			Nothing to note.	
	19/6/16	10 a.m.	Cpln BERRY to report to around 25 Div. to listening duty to returns. Lt. HEATH reverted from leave.	
	20/6/16	3 pm	Cpln PATRICK left fr. England his contract having expired.	
	21/6/16	10 a.m.	Lt. GRANT RG R.A. reports here to duty to relieve at KHANDAHAR FARM lines visit orders to A.D.S. Trois Rois -	
		3 pm	Capt MOIR out to relieve Cpln HAY on Trois Rois.	
	22/6/16	10 a.m.	Lunch to KHANDAHAR FARM – Trois Rois + Ba--	
		3 pm	Cpn HAY moved on 10 days leave.	
	23/6/16	11 am	Cpln BERRY returns from 25 Divi.	
	24/6/16	3 pm	S.M. WCATEER proceeds on leave to 10 days.	

WAR DIARY
or
INTELLIGENCE SUMMARY

(Erase heading not required.)

Army Form C. 2118

Place	Date	Hour	Summary of Events and Information	Remarks and references to Appendices
13/11/16	24/10	3pm	Capn HENNESSY detailed to return H.O. 8-R.99 - proceeding on leave	
	28/10	3pm	Visited Trois Ponts & B-etts & paid men civic employees	
		2pm	Visiter officer Pont-Pin- Pont-Molle-	
	29/10	—	acting adviser work of Ypres area - Asst O. Moore to drew no. mon	
	29/10	4	Reg. for Pate came to tea	
	30/10	10am	Inspection Klondike farm - Haw Park - Red Barn -	

R.H. Dunn Overton
Lt. Col. cmndt.
Y. 1105 - 9 Am.

140/9

5th D

110th Field Ambulance.

Dec 1916

Army Form C. 2118

WAR DIARY
or
INTELLIGENCE SUMMARY
(Erase heading not required.)

110th Field Ambulance   Vol / 5

Instructions regarding War Diaries and Intelligence Summaries are contained in F. S. Regs., Part II. and the Staff Manual respectively. Title Pages will be prepared in manuscript.

Place	Date	Hour	Summary of Events and Information	Remarks and references to Appendices
BAILLEUL	1/7/16	11 am	Visit KHANDAHAR FARM.	
	2/7/16	3 pm	Maj. D.Q.M.G. (General RYCROFT) from S.H.Q. came to inspect the Bullets.	
	3/7/16	6 pm	Capt. BERRY arrived to relieve H.D. 12. N.S.R. ordered proceeds to HAZEBROUCK in a	
	4/7/16	6 am	first keep ammo to ammunition.	
	5/7/16	10 am	Capt. HAY received from leave.	
		3 pm	Capt. HAY received to duty at Trois Arcs & Post	
	6/7/16	6 am	Col. MOIR returns to Rind grounds. A dressing inspected and examined	
			S.M. McATEER received from leave.	
	7/7/16		Visit KHANDAHAR FARM – Trois Arcs, Post – Cas. HENNESY Posts & Dr.	
	8/7/16	10 am	Occupied Rearing to advanced Dressing Station posts.	
	9/7/16	10 am	Capt. DOW & Lt. GLANVILLE report their arrival for duty	
			Capt. BERRY received from 12 A.G.R.	
		11 am	Capt. MOIR went to relieve Mr. GRANT at KHANDAHAR FARM	
	10/7/16	11 am	Capt. BERRY proceeds to 172 Bde A.T.A. as M.O.C.	
		3 pm	Lt. GLANVILLE proceeds to relieve M.O. of N.S.R. who proceeds on course	
			to Sanitation.	
	11/7/16	10 am	Event appointment to A.G.C.M. & Cpl. Ep. SHEEHY & D. McKEE.	
	12/7/16		Nothing to relieve.	

WAR DIARY
or
INTELLIGENCE SUMMARY
(Erase heading not required.)

Army Form C. 2118

Place	Date	Hour	Summary of Events and Information	Remarks and references to Appendices
BAILLEUL	13/7/16	—	Noting to add	
	14/7/16	10am	Lieut C. T. RHANDHAR FARM – Trois Noirs Baton.	
	15/7/16	11am	Cpt S KELLY, D. McKee attd by F.G.C.M.	
	16/7/16	5pm	Lt. GLANVILLE arrived to lead escort.	
	17/7/16	4pm	Cpt Don arr & revise Cpt MOIR to KANDAHAR FARM – & to relieve Bttn on being relieved & proceed to Hyde Park Corner & relieve	
			M.O. 10 - Lunchinge & proceed 6 - Hyde Bunch for a Coran X Same item.	
	18/7/16	4pm	Proceed part events of F.G.C.M on Cpt Kelly, D. McKee.	
	19/7/16	2.02	Arrived inspect H.Q of G.O.C., Inns Linen.	
	20/7/16	4pm	Lt. McKee on ard to RPM & arrived 3 nimp F.P. N°1	
	21/7/16	10am	Inspect Rhodes arm. Limi noin Batt.	
	22/7/16	10am	Inspect Offui nom Bill Hmt Moris.	
	23/7/16	10am	S.M. Mc ATEER proceed to Exped rating to Catn relieve pris & Tring a Lefang Comean.	
	24/7/16	11am	A. GLANVILLE relied from the 5 - N.G.N.	

Army Form C. 2118

WAR DIARY
or
INTELLIGENCE SUMMARY
(Erase heading not required.)

Instructions regarding War Diaries and Intelligence Summaries are contained in F.S. Regs., Part II. and the Staff Manual respectively. Title Pages will be prepared in manuscript.

Place	Date	Hour	Summary of Events and Information	Remarks and references to Appendices
BAILLEUL	25/7/16	9 am	Cpl. McPATRICK reports him evacuated from the lines for injury. Stores are now being & are now the same as those previous.	
"	26/7/16	10 am	Lt. GLANVILLE proceeds to 172 Bde N.Z.A. to relieve Capt. BERRY, the latter returning in exchange due to no cause.	
"	27/7/16	1 pm	Heavy rain made us sedentary of the departure for the lines.	
"	28/7/16		Heavy rain.	
"	29/7/16	10 am	Cpl. MOIR proceeds to relieve Cpl. Henning proceeding on leave to M.O. 36. D.A.C.	
		11 am	Lt. Cpl. CHRISTIE to visit the Canadian Camps. He will bring for 10 days with M.O. friends on leave.	
"	30/7/16	3 pm	Attended meeting of Mess. Smith 2nd Army at REMY Siding. Arranged on a visit to Officer Nurs. State. MONT NOIR	

B.H. Weer mann
Lt. Col. mann
y. 110: R. Amn. C.

36

140/943

No 2 Light Ambulance

36 hrs

COMMITTEE FOR THE
MEDICAL HISTORY OF THE WAR
Date 13 MAR 1917

WAR DIARY
or
INTELLIGENCE SUMMARY.

Army Form C. 2118.

Place	Date	Hour	Summary of Events and Information	Remarks and references to Appendices
BAILLEUL	1/7	6.30am	OC Shepherd & Asst proceed to Eques & a casto[?] train being offered to Cannes.	
	"	3pm	ADMS made an inspection of 2.A.M.R., Home Lines.	
	2/7	10am	Paid a visit to Hazebrouck Pond – Yarra Pen & Baths.	
		2pm	Paid over to 7.A.	
	3/7	10am	In newspaper ministry – Shot & prisoners present.	
	4/7	"	Writing to mich[?]	
	5/7	3pm	Attended divine service in B.² I.C.C.S.	
	6/7	10am	On decision being received from Corps Gen BERRY & company returned	
			to HQ 9.A. & reports[?] his visit this morning.	
	7/7	3pm	Aeroplanes 15 Osiers to Mount Pris & cinde an inspection	
	8/7	9am	Gen BERRY proceed to Hazebrand for a time & then to	
			I.N.C.O.'s & now reports to D.H. & Sea. Prail & – so by carr &	
			Smilton.	
				R.H.Deen Lieut
				fr. M Lemere
	"	3pm	Proceed on 21 days leave.	

WAR DIARY
or
INTELLIGENCE SUMMARY.
(Erase heading not required.)

Army Form C. 2118.

Place	Date	Hour	Summary of Events and Information	Remarks and references to Appendices
BAILLEUL	9/7	—	Lt Col DUNBAR, D.C. proceeded on 21 days leave yesterday	
	13/7	2pm	Cpn MOIR arrived from Boulogne Hosp. via 10 DRS	
		2pm	Cpn BERRY arrived from 2nd Army Souv X Saud Testi.	
	16/7	2pm	Cpn MOIR and to relieve Cpn HAY in Trois Bois - the latter to relieve Cpn EMERSON on 10 days leave.	
	17/7	2pm	Cpn EMERSON proceeded on 10 days leave to Ireland.	
	18/7	10am	Rev. S. HAYES C.F. reported his arrival being posted to this unit for duty.	
	20/7	2pm	Cpn W.S. BERRY proceeded on 10 days leave to Ireland	
	30/7	11am	Lt Col DUNBAR arrived from leave.	
				W E Patrick Capt R.A.M.C.
	31/7	10am	Returned from leave last night. Cpn EMERSON arrived from leave + proceed to Officers Rest House MONT NOIR.	B. Lt Colin Dunbar Lt Col comdy # 105 F. A.

140/1997

COMMITTEE FOR THE
MEDICAL HISTORY OF THE WAR
Date 4 - APR.1917

36th Div.

110th Field Ambulance

Feb.1917

WAR DIARY or INTELLIGENCE SUMMARY

Army Form C. 2118

110 3rd Aug Vol 17

Place	Date	Hour	Summary of Events and Information	Remarks and references to Appendices
BAILLEUL	1/7	10am	Capt HAY on being relieved at MONT NOIR returns to Trois Rois.	
		12 m	Capt MOIR returns to Headquarters from Trois Rois.	
	2/7	10am	Capt BERRY returns from leave — He is temporarily posted to 1/15 Middx Regt.	
			Capt GLANVILLE transferred to 1st 109 F.A.	
			Capt BERRY proceeded to 9: Corps H.Q. & men & dressers being chosen & detained in turn.	
	4/7	10.30	Pte AGNUS made an inspection of the H.Q. of the units.	
		3pm	Accompanied Lt AGNUS to MONT NOIR.	
	5/7	6am	Capt MOIR proceeds on 10 days leave to MARSEILLES Italy.	
	6/7	10am	Visited KHANDAHAR FARM — Trois Rois Batt.	
		3pm	AGNUS came to inspect horse men chosen to & keeping inspect.	
	7/7	10am	Accompanied Col Lessey on an inspection to the Dressing Room, found all in order. Paid men at Hd Quarters.	
	8/7	1pm	Seven men to pay men over statements.	
	9/7	10am	Leave also on visit to 62 KHANDAHAR FARM to receive the ordinary party 108 F.A. back to 1st in Headquarters.	

WAR DIARY
or
INTELLIGENCE SUMMARY.

(Erase heading not required.)

Army Form C. 2118.

Place	Date	Hour	Summary of Events and Information	Remarks and references to Appendices
BAILLEUL	10/7	10 am	Entering Party of 10th F.A. reports to H.Q. units.	
		3 pm	Men from H.Q. hunting by request of Hardouin's Farm	
		10 pm	Manga arrived from Capt Hay. 1st Cpl. Dow was Town sic on	
	11/7		KHANDAHAR FARM. Sent Cpl. PATRICK to visit Cpl. DOW.	
	12/7	3 pm	Cpl. DOW was evacuated to No. 2 C.C.S. N.Y.D. ABDOMINAL.	
		10 am	Went to see Cpl. DOW at No. 2 C.C.S. – Report ? his abdomen.	
	13/7	10 am	Apparent recovery of wounds.	
			Brigade moved. 1st Cpl. DOW to have evacuated 1/7 Bnn.	
	15/7	8 am	The New HAYES .C.F. attended No. 2 A Procvd to 8 OMER. Gased	
			by Sen Chaplain to H. Div.	
	16/7	9 am	Pte STRICKLAND – 13 R.G.R. buged this morning from A.D.S. W.F.G.S.W.	
			hand – & died soon aft our we here. Clairmy repeats in H	
			usual way.	
	17/7	8 am	Then Influenzic flee carried into	
	18/7	3 pm	Dis'd a visit to Officers Mess French.	
	19/7	11 am	Visits Rondelm Farm, Trois Bois – All service.	

WAR DIARY
or
INTELLIGENCE SUMMARY.
(Erase heading not required.)

Army Form C. 2118.

Place	Date	Hour	Summary of Events and Information	Remarks and references to Appendices
BAILLEUL	20/7	7am	Opened relies in attempt on & troops arrived by the evening news)	
			today - Raining 6 met	
	21/7	—		
	22/7	8am	The Rev. MAYSE C.F. visits today from 21 Divn.	
		10am	Capt. MOIR visits from our today.	
	23/7	10am	Capt. MOIR returned to parent today to KANDAHAR FARM for duty	
			to review Capt. PATRICK. The latter to remain 6th Bn. Runners.	
	24/7	10am	Capt. BERRY visits 6 H.Q. today from 14 Coys —	
		11am	Arrang. made an impress of H.Q. Mess Room & kitchen.	
	25/7	10am	Paid a visit to Mont Noir O.R.S. & 1st Capt. PATRICK anxious	
			but to am no M.O. accompanying having to attend one Sick Room	
			EMERSON is laid up.	
	26/7	4pm	Gen. Hunters Brics. Insp. Rest today —	
	27/7	10am	Inspects KANDAHAR FAR, TROIS ROIS & BAILL.	
		3/-	Inspects O.R.S. MONT NOIR.	
	28/7	4pm	Capt. CHRISTIE proceeds on 10 days casual leave today	
			R. in. seen annex H. Cie reserve Yr. no: L.Q.	

36th Div

110th Field Ambulance

14C/2042

COMMITTEE FOR THE
MEDICAL HISTORY OF THE WAR
Date 11 MAY 1917

Army Form C. 2118.

WAR DIARY
or
INTELLIGENCE SUMMARY.
(Erase heading not required.)

110 Yd Amb_e

Vol / 8

Instructions regarding War Diaries and Intelligence Summaries are contained in F. S. Regs., Part II. and the Staff Manual respectively. Title pages will be prepared in manuscript.

Place	Date	Hour	Summary of Events and Information	Remarks and references to Appendices
BAILLEUL	1/3/17	—	Meeting of unit	
"	2/3/17	9am	Cpl GLANVILLE arrived for 2 days from 1st in O.S.9. R. M.O. & RE	
			union trenches arrived from trenches	
"	3/3/17	3pm	Paid a visit to A & O.R.S. MONT NOIR	
"	4/3/17	3pm	Orders went on inspection to H.Q & F.A.	
"	5/3/17	3pm	went to ADS TROIS ROIS & on Cpl HAY.	
"	6/3/17	3pm	On return pried had listing. Snow falling today.	
"	7/3/17	10am	Cpl PATRICK arrived to C.H.Q. from MONT NOIR	
"	8/3/17	11am	Sent Cpl BERRY to relieve Cpl MOIR who is this afternoon leaving	
			on paid. H.Q. found by the Div Gen Officer.	
"		12pm	went to MONT NOIR. Paid visit	
"	8/3/17	3pm	Paid visit to KANDAHAR – TROIS ROIS & MONT NOIR	
"	9/3/17	4pm	Cpl GLANVILLE sent to relieve Cpl CORNEY at R.J.Q. when he will not be known	
			from "	
"	10/3/17	3pm	Orders & inspected H.Q. 1am lorries & Bicycle	
"	11/3/17	2pm	Inspected Officer from Staff – Green – Mann .	

WAR DIARY
or
INTELLIGENCE SUMMARY.
(Erase heading not required.)

Army Form C. 2118.

Place	Date	Hour	Summary of Events and Information	Remarks and references to Appendices
BAILLEUL	12/7	10am	Inspected KANDAHAR FARM — Trois Rois + Batt.	
		3pm	Capt MAYBERRY returned from leave from 15 Rein.	
			O.O. received on leaving on J KANDAHAR FARM C Men leaves Rein	
"	13/7	11am	Met O.C. + N°3 F.A. New General sic to KANDAHAR FARM & arranged about the handing over	
"	14/7	10am	Sent 15 Q.M. to meet 15 Q.M. + to arrange re-receiving F.A. & hand over equipment on to KANDAHAR FARM.	
"	15/7	10am	Handed over A.D.S. KANDAHAR FARM & N°3 New Zealand F.A. between units C.H.Q.	
"	16/7	10am	Handed over PALMER BATHS 15 New Zealand Div. Between Div. between units C.H.Q.	
"	"	3pm	Handed over the Cinema to MONT NOIR C to 1X Corps.	
"	17/7	10am	Handed over R.A.Ds TROIS ROIS & 0.01 New Zealand F.A. between units C.H.Q.	
"	18/7			

WAR DIARY or INTELLIGENCE SUMMARY

Army Form C. 2118.

Place	Date	Hour	Summary of Events and Information	Remarks and references to Appendices
BAILLEUL	19/2/17	3 pm	Received orders C^ had 1 Officer & undertaken C^ wards with about half inch mis 150 109 Bde & 5th Training Cadre.	
"	20/2/17	9 am	2 Lieut C. French rendered Capt EMERSON to the Bde. Lieut CROSSLEY temporarily attached by the Armed C^ pending C. French for instruction.	
"	21/2/17	3 pm	C. French report 1st [illeg.] Capt MAYO & Lt SAY reported to duty in C. of g R.L. Dominion winter sports having report &	
"	22/2/17	10 am	Camp received by Lieut-Col Pritchard. Capt MAYBERRY returns & reports for duty mi–14. 109 F.A. in [illeg.] [illeg.] – L. MORRIS.	
"	23/2/17	2 pm	Lt LINDSAY from Army Artillery & reports here for duty. Adms Bonsand make an inspect & H.R. Faulkner have been & viewed.	
"	25/2/17	3 am	Visited Cap. HAY C. on Code & Employed Sections & hoop campfires by Company Orderly Constable.	
"	26/2/17	3 am	Lieut CHRISTIE C. reviewed now & to Asen. Aid Party on his lemon Cypress Road.	
"	27/2/17	10 am	Lemon setting C. ac C. French to BOULDEN AUSTN. Received ––	

WAR DIARY
or
INTELLIGENCE SUMMARY

(Erase heading not required.)

Army Form C. 2118.

Place	Date	Hour	Summary of Events and Information	Remarks and references to Appendices
BAILLEUL	28/5/17	10 am	Leave Camp occupied by 33rd Bgy R.F.A. & parts Pk.t & amn.	
"	29/5/17	—	6" actions	
"	30/5/17	10 am	Writing & misc. Accepted ordered to stand — rain — to be drawing first for training camp.	
"	31/5/17	9 am	Lot. & M.S. Officer IX Corps & had w/C to him & meeting an officer from Fate —	
			O.O. recd. re taking over batts. in DRANOUTRE fm 111/109 R.A.	
		4 pm	Capt. N.E. PATRICK man. was on sickness & fever to	
			ey. Evans to N°. 2 C.C.S.	
			Capt. BERRY appointed tem. 2nd Officer	

13.14 Jean Demeter
Lt. Col. Namur
Yc 1105 R.A.

3
31/17

140/2086

COMMITTEE FOR THE
MEDICAL HISTORY OF THE WAR
Date −6 JUN. 1917

110^R 7 a.

WAR DIARY or INTELLIGENCE SUMMARY

Army Form C. 2118.

110 2n Auf

Vol 19

Place	Date	Hour	Summary of Events and Information	Remarks and references to Appendices
BAILLEUL	1/7/19	9 am	Orders received re billeting our batt. in DRANOUTRE	
"	2/7/19	9 am	Cpn. HAY and 1 NCO & 9 men went to the new Billets from K 109 - F.A.	
"	"	2 pm	Sent 1 NCO & 9 men to relieve similar party of K 105 - F.A.	
			Working party for 170 Coy R.E.	
"	3/7/19	2 pm	Sent 1 NCO & 10 men to relieve similar party of K 105 F.A. at its hiring Camp.	
		2.30h	Attended Conference at DDMS office to discuss questions re experience	
"	4/7/19	11 am	Agent reports HQ F.A. Transport & Billets	
		2 pm	Rearpois agreed to whom aim to training would come. Billets for BAILLEUL - LOCRE Road.	
			Capt. BEERY goes to 9 Corps headquaters to inspect trg. Paid visit -	
"	5/7/19	3 pm	Inspect Billets at DRANOUTRE	
	6/7/19	3 pm	C. Section returns from BOUVEKERQUE - being sick K 109 Rgt.	
	7/7/19	9 am	Drake arrangements to resume sick from 10r Bn - Bertin Lenn	
	8/7/19	11.30am	Capt. H.O. to his Bureau disposed of HQ 105 Rgt -	
	9/7/19	2 pm	En. Herman Paid here his...	
			Sent 8 men to replace K 105 F.A. as - entering party of Kinderhoek	
	10/7/19	10 am	Cpn. MOIR. 1 NCO & 5 men sent to Satin heard at CAESTRE	
	11/7/19	10 am	to return	

WAR DIARY
INTELLIGENCE SUMMARY

Army Form C. 2118.

Place	Date	Hour	Summary of Events and Information	Remarks and references to Appendices
BRIGUL	11/7/17	2.30pm	Lieut. I.N.Co. & men to look after sick Burton & L. Bosier & troops	
"		10pm	Cpl BURTON R.A.M.C. reports his arrival & party from ROUEN. Taken on the strength.	
"	12/7/17	5.30 pm	D.M.S. 2nd Army inspects I.C. F.A. Hsting.	
"	13/7/17	10 am	Cpl EMERSON & Cpl BURTON & to NCO's house & to transport personnel	
"			Hstg wire I.C. 107 Bde & I.C. training area.	
"	16/7/17	3pm	Lieut. I.N.Co & 3 men & I.C. Ammunition School at BETHUNE to see units inspection	
"		5pm	Cpl GLANVILLE reports I.C. F.A. from I.C. 157 R.A.P on the removal of	
"			Cpl CORKEY from their aid dump.	
"	18/7/17	10 am	Arrives made on inspection I.C. F.A. stores Louis & Pericens.	
"		2pm	Q.M. HEATH sees C.C.C.L. outgoing from Hsp return Lislubut	
"	19/7/17	2pm	Inducing party attacks C. 107 F.A. arrives from Lislubut.	
"			Arriving 6 men	
"	21/7/17	—	Fire recd from M.L.C.C.L saying I.C. Off & R.M.L. HEATH had	
"	22/7/17	11 am	been recalled to the Base	
"			Cpl W.S. BERRY rejoins I.C. F.A. & I.C. take up appointment of Orderly Corp.	
"	24/7/17	2pm	W.D. shews the strength of I.C. F.A.	
"		11am	Lieut Douglas with I.C. 107 Bde & L. WATTING.	
"	27/7/17	—	Lieut MOIR joining 10 days special leave to GRENOBLE.	

Army Form C. 2118.

WAR DIARY
or
INTELLIGENCE SUMMARY

(Erase heading not required.)

Instructions regarding War Diaries and Intelligence Summaries are contained in F. S. Regs., Part II. and the Staff Manual respectively. Title Pages will be prepared in manuscript.

Place	Date	Hour	Summary of Events and Information	Remarks and references to Appendices
BAILLEUL	29/1	11 a.m.	Davis + Hopper transp to manage & 15th corr Office Post Field in 15 Rue D'Ypres. Captn QUANTIELS for the day.	
"	30/1	11 am	Arnold went on inspect to 15 this Ardenne. No news to write any kay events from the enemy. Both men Francois & Jury. 15.10. Seen Doctor Lt. Cl. name O/C 110 - F. Anse	

140/216

No. 110. F.A.

COMMITTEE FOR THE
MEDICAL HISTORY OF THE WAR
Date 10 JUL. 1917

May 1917

War Diary / Intelligence Summary

Army Form C. 2118.

110 2nd Aust

Vol 2

Place	Date	Hour	Summary of Events and Information	Remarks and references to Appendices
BAILLEUL	1/5/17	7am	Troops moved to camp & spent the effects from past to the reception of prisoners.	
		12 n	Orders received to supply two officers. One that it was mostly tried to establish reporting to Capt EMERSON to report for reconn. & spare. Such troops.	
			C/manner change of the Effects from state.	
	2/5/17	3p	Capt BURTON & 7E acts with 7C 117 Bde awaiting C.R.E. orders from	
			training area.	
	3/5/17	3pm	Paraded to F.J.A.	
	4/5/17	3pm	training & bath.	
			Sent 1 NCO & 20 men to 100 R.A. & 20 men to 100 R.A. Prisoners & received by Pte R.A. Reserve.	N.A.P. or (Ind.) unrefs?
	5/5/17	11am	D.ADMS TR troops inspected R.R.A. Reserve.	
	6/5/17	1 am	Sent 1 Hand Car & party to be attached to 15th B.R. during	
			their day in front line for draw taking.	
	7/5/17	noon	Recvd telephone message & arrange for taking in the O.R.S.	
			at 15. 19 = Div.	
	8/5/17	1 pm	Went up to meet Bois at N 31 C 5.7.3. to give necessary orders	
			to bearing contacts. The event to assist operation.	
		upon	Passed to Advance Bearer at D.A.Q in an attack to stretcher	
			of Casualties in the firing Army.	

2449 Wt. W14957/Mgo 750,000 1/16 J.B.C. & A. Forms/C.2118/12.

WAR DIARY
or
INTELLIGENCE SUMMARY

(Erase heading not required.)

Army Form C. 2118.

Place	Date	Hour	Summary of Events and Information	Remarks and references to Appendices
BAILLEUL	11/7	10 am	Wire received from I.C. N Gden Section that G.S. of 27 Div Australians. Capt MUIR left me from Gen. Convoy at Aubigny & Australians.	
"	"	2 pm	Moved on IX Corps BRS L. 19. Brig. & replies received to Australs.	
"	12/7	9 am	First Batch 10 men & evening party to LINDENHOEK	
"	13/7	noon	Others moved on run of DH.Q. holding reports & movement of men & convoys	
"	14/7	1 am	Cpl. CAHOUN reached 6 prisoners at his own request not to contain but by C. Monett	
"	15/7	9 am	Cpl. BURTON proceeded on 14 days contact leave.	
"	"	noon	About 10 men sent to LINDENHOEK in evening party. Shown motor-bike & 50 men to LINDENHOEK M.D.H.Q.	
"	16/7	9 am	Attached medley of O.C.'s M.D.S. DRANOUTRE head by the Supt. of M.O. Sta.	
"	"	11am	bore the aroused of Billins in M.D.S. DRANOUTRE, when bur in 15 Hon It and of evening convoy to LINDENHOEK M.O.S.t evening convoy in L.C. Also saw 15 from others.	
"	18/7	10 am	"I write and bury arrangement" Capt EMERSON & HAY take at The Crue laken to accomodate The numbers of contains concerned. Ren Car 15 Dr. Orwin. 6 B.R.C. Posing.	

WAR DIARY or INTELLIGENCE SUMMARY

Army Form C. 2118.

Place	Date	Hour	Summary of Events and Information	Remarks and references to Appendices
BAILLEUL	19/5	3pm	Attended Conference at Brigade Office	
"	21/5	10 am	Sent up parties to N.B. C.L.S. to prepare camp & draw essentials prior to arrival of unit(?)	
"	22/5	11 am	Went to the end point on the arrival camp to meet incoming unit.	
"	23/5	10 am	Attended meeting with O.C. S.R.E.C.Y. Em?? O.C. No. 4 Division Train & Brigade to co-ordinate details re arrival & coming — BAILLEUL	
"	24/5	3pm	XX Div. 18 Ardres & Ardres moved. Good covering part & coming	
"	25/7	10am	Wen to N.D.C.B.S.L.? reported arriving & arranged a? to mention at 15 ord. Supply	
"	26/5	—	for K. evening Convoy — awaiting to see.	
"	27/5	12 m	Arrange issue to D.R.L.S.? R.A. for the Convoy & 2 coms to Eng & Army? one 14 R 's accommodation	
"	28/5	10am	Capt. Hay toured our Br? & Ser Hosp. DRANOUTRE to see the premises to be used as R.M.store. Arrived 145 to Army.	
"	29/5	3pm	Capt. Moir to party from Sudor Hospital to CROISTREL beyond last convoy there.	
"	"	7pm	Orders received to send an officer to renew Capt. CORKEY late N.D.O.7 Capt. HAY detailed for the duty.	

WAR DIARY
or
INTELLIGENCE SUMMARY

(Erase heading not required.)

Army Form C. 2118.

Place	Date	Hour	Summary of Events and Information	Remarks and references to Appendices
BAILLEUL	30/5/17	1pm	Return received of recruits sent from 107 Bde in the BERTHEN AREA	
"	31/5/17	11am	Capt BURTON received O/F Court Enquiry.	
		5pm	G Party of 1 O R was missing on LINDENHOEK area is Wulvergem Enemy.	

31/5/17

A.H. Deep ?
Lt. Col. R.M.C.
O/c 110? F.A.

140/230

COMMITTEE FOR THE
MEDICAL HISTORY OF THE WAR
Date - 7 AUG 1917

No 110 7.A.

June 1917
Pam/S

WAR DIARY

Army Form C. 2118.

INTELLIGENCE SUMMARY

(Erase heading not required.)

Place	Date	Hour	Summary of Events and Information	Remarks and references to Appendices
BAILLEUL	1/9/17	—	Major (Temp M.C.O.) B.H.V. DUNBAR — Capt W.S. BHAY, Kenin & Pte R. STRICKLAND. This visit is to inspect — Paid out + was ready for further any Instr.	
"	2/9/17	9 pm 10 am	Capt MOIR & BURTON went up to the line. No firing at will.	
"	3/9/17	—		
"	4/9/17	10 am 11 am	Drew one H.D. horse from Divisional Artillery. Arms inspection. The Remainder of 15 R.A. Inf. equipped to 1 NCO + + 8 O.R. has been on evening practice in N°1 R.E.G. Young Officers comparison. Three on the field over.	
"	"	5:30 pm	Detail carriers + others 1X men O.C. arranged with Mining Corp to put out in areas + some powder.	
"	5/9/17 6/9/17	— 12 am	Arrangements every listening + lis one + letters from evacuation to the evacuating point of evening could be on the advance in evening. The	
"	"	3 pm 7 pm	The main body arrived in Armenia, officers, others ranks and horses. After spending the next day. Seven men have been killed. under Capt BURTON & 2/Lt D.I.S. RAP and Report here arrived Capt MOIR & 2/Lt PARKER.	

WAR DIARY or INTELLIGENCE SUMMARY

Army Form C. 2118.

(Erase heading not required.)

Instructions regarding War Diaries and Intelligence Summaries are contained in F. S. Regs., Part II. and the Staff Manual respectively. Title Pages will be prepared in manuscript.

Place	Date	Hour	Summary of Events and Information	Remarks and references to Appendices
Bailleul	6/1/17	8 pm	at S.P. 6. Capt Brimelow with 15 men of 15 R.A. 3 late wt my pickets on N31 & 3.57. Reconnoitering Party for Battery locations. Guide to Capt CORNEY who was detailed to move to 15 Squadron this was necessary anticipation in event of enemy breakdown of breastworks & float.	
N31. e.s.s.	7/1/17	9.30 h 3.10 am	3 Flare Relation of 15, 107 R.A. Rouvrey's hope is Eleanor's Rear line, announced by 15 captains & anon 5. Accuracy & moral 3 anon. fires by some activities in our positions. The firing continued. April 15 enemy batteries in enemy country. The pickets over nature. The enemy were seen by 15 Y.M.C.A. + they out our fire not...	
"		6 AM	Roy 15 & Capt 15 was about to by supplies in the new front army lost by the Listening Posts to be advanced to O.C. TR Col. Kepsi Gs examined the wire and listed properly. Rain for 15 minutes to wet...	
"		6.30	Lewis action 6 hours, of 3 min shown. 15 minute 6c over 6-8.3 from intervals on 15 snipers & genie..	

M.G.C.S. Army Nov 1916

2449 Wt. W14957/M90 750,000 1/16 J.B.C. & A. Forms/C.2118/12.

Army Form C. 2118.

WAR DIARY
or
INTELLIGENCE SUMMARY
(Erase heading not required.)

Instructions regarding War Diaries and Intelligence Summaries are contained in F. S. Regs., Part II. and the Staff Manual respectively. Title Pages will be prepared in manuscript.

Place	Date	Hour	Summary of Events and Information	Remarks and references to Appendices
M 31 c 5.5.	7/7/17	10.45 am	Reported to [Bty] that there was not between [...] of [Canadian] Fd Amm Col. As the [...] morning I took over from [...] handed over [...] battalion.	L. Cooper was 2/Lt D.; L. Robertson 2/Lt [...]
		8.30 am	Reported to D.I.M. CCS	
			Troops arrived L: and 1. [Ryan] attached L: [...] R.A.P. 9th 3 (Reports that) J - B. [Ryan] stationed at 15th 109 F.A. under Cpl. DAVIDSON in [...]	
		12.15 pm	Expects 23 ams L: BERTHEN. I. also [...] camp.	
		5 pm	Troops [arrive] from Cpl MUIR L: enq his men are getting when his [...] of [...] from L: Robins of [...] 1. Been [...] of 15: 109: F.A. under Cpl. HART, an [...] at	
		9 pm	Amu[...] no am [...]	
M	8/7/17	12.30 am	Amu[...] arrived L: and [...] of [...] [...] [...] Cpl. BURTON [...] [...] [...] [...] [...]	

WAR DIARY
or
INTELLIGENCE SUMMARY

(Erase heading not required.)

Army Form C. 2118.

Place	Date	Hour	Summary of Events and Information	Remarks and references to Appendices
M.31.c.35	8/7	4 a.m.	of the 109. F.A. under Cpt. RUSSELL on return met & Cpt. BURTON and his men went to Westoutre for a rest. Arrangements made & 1st men to proceed to trenches at the evening to relieve C/15. Pnr. G 2 & 3 Pltn Report Centres beginning to entrench on A.O.S. Rd. near C/15' Officers now being briefed.	
		4pm	Capt. Stephen to Bn Gnrs. Engineers to [illegible]	C-M.2.2 r.3
		1pm	2nd in Cmd. Cpt. GLANVILLE & Cdr.Sey. & 13. O.R. to proceed to LINDENHOEK.	
			Reports that they met & various 15cm guns in A.O.S.	
		3pm	J moved L on A.O.S. to Report Centres & to LINDENHOEK w/o incident L- Return to camp.	
		4pm	Cpt. MOIR & his Bomb. Section ready to Bn guarters.	
		6pm	Orders received to move up to LINDENHOEK. Stop to allow camp.	
		9pm	Lyn NJ/6.3.35. J moved my [illegible] to proceed L- LINDENHOEK & report. a runner from Cpt. MOIR to Bn HQ ord /Lts camp. Lt on AOS LINDENHOEK & entered in a firm during	
LINDENHOEK		10.pm	[illegible] rain L- across 35. Run	
		10.30 pm		

Army Form C. 2118.

WAR DIARY
or
INTELLIGENCE SUMMARY

(Erase heading not required.)

Instructions regarding War Diaries and Intelligence Summaries are contained in F. S. Regs., Part II and the Staff Manual respectively. Title Pages will be prepared in manuscript.

Place	Date	Hour	Summary of Events and Information	Remarks and references to Appendices
LINDENHOEK	6/1/17	10.30 pm	Advised by TR that supply 1st 9 L.I. trench & mortar bn lorries etc.	
			are lying over an hour's drive down from HQs repair photo to 1st 105 F.A. at DRANOUTRE. Lorries are on their way & received C⁰ O.'s 11 card by Orderly.	
	9/1/17	8 am	Very few new arrivals. Troops leaving the trijou.	
		9.30 am	Oct. 3⁰. S⁰. F.A. & Section 1/1 Div. Canad. hrs. to rendezvous with L₁- bn to moving men & by lorries & am the NCO's viv.-15 dismounts	
			1st Sec.	
		3 pm	Advanced party of 13th F.A. arrived.	
		7 am	Sent out 40 men to relieve & ambulance members of Platoon	
			Reeve of 1st 109. F.A.	
		9 pm	Relief lorries arrived & brom C⁰ B.O.C.C.J.S. to 1st major, 1st L.-	
			numbers of relief.	
10/1/17	1 am	Officers arr. ready on the tactical C⁰ N- 13. F.A. was...	
			a relief lorries C⁰ BATISSON & all relief are men army continuous	
			Camp, ie BERTHEN	
			from the 13. F.A. Brand C⁰ arrive	

WAR DIARY or INTELLIGENCE SUMMARY

Army Form C. 2118.

(Erase heading not required.)

Instructions regarding War Diaries and Intelligence Summaries are contained in F. S. Regs., Part II. and the Staff Manual respectively. Title Pages will be prepared in manuscript.

Place	Date	Hour	Summary of Events and Information	Remarks and references to Appendices
LINDENHOEK	10/6/17	10.15 am	Relieved 36 & and officers & 1st 35th F.A. wounded & one and 1st Depot's a/c - bn - to receiving and 1st Devon Beachcross.	
		9.45 pm	Relieving completed. Patrol to ex of junction H.Q. to BAILLEUL.	
BAILLEUL	11/6/17	10.30	Report Inspection & analysis & Army 36.	
		9.30 am	Orders C. Pools under Capt EMERSON & Lieut & BERTHEN & 1st an 18 Bar entrance camps from 33rd F.A.	
		10 am	Lunch then by way & on the phone	
		12 n	Camp later no 3 report quarter & reserve & 1st Depot	
		3 pm	line receive & meet Capt GLANVILLE & reserve M.O. at N.T.M.	
	12/6/17	10 am	Report Capt CORREY fit & duty:	
		5 pm	Capt CORREY reviews 1st 1st N.T.M., Capt HAY, reviews him on being relieved.	
	13/6/17	9 am	Capt HAY & 2 N.C.O.s & 10 men & reserve & M. Team CARRELL to the men laundry for Q and & join & few days training the evening & arrears	
	"	3 pm	Proceed on 10 days leave	

B.H. Green
J.C. Lussen

WAR DIARY or INTELLIGENCE SUMMARY

Army Form C. 2118.

Place	Date	Hour	Summary of Events and Information	Remarks and references to Appendices
Bailleul	13/6/17	2 pm	IX Corps Convalescent Camp Bartle handed over by Capt Emerson to O.C. 58th F.A. 19th Divn	
"	13/6/17	2.20 pm	The O.C. 58th F.A. sent in 2.20 proceeded on 10 days leave to England. Capt Blondin RAMC Assuming Command of the Unit.	
"	"	3 pm	Capt Hay with 2 N.C.O + 10 men reported here for duty, their work having been completed at Belle Ostan Capple.	
"	"	3.45 pm	Capt Emerson with 6 section reports the arrival from Battle apts leaving in Convalescent Camp.	
"	"		Capt Emerson assumed command of the Ambulance from Capt & Prieu.	
"	"		Capt Moir was detached + proceeded to IX Corps Cardiac Hospital Cassel (instructions SDMS 1 X Corps) The message from H.M. The King to G in C. was read to all ranks on parade duly with the Captain B	
"	14/6/17	10 am	MESSINES + especially work done by R.A.M.C.	
"	"	2 pm	Col Eng CMG. AMS ADMS 36th Divn inspected the Hospital, Billets &c.	
"	15/6/17	11 am	Capt E. MERDAM with 8 B other ranks proceeded to 109th F.A. for institution + to be thanked by Surgeon General Pike D.M.S. II Army, for work in the recent operation. 22 following officers reported the Surgeon General — the ADMS + DADMS. IX Corps + the ADMS + a/DADMS 36th Divn	
"	16/6/17	2 pm	Capt Eric G. LINDSAY R.A.M.C. was detailed + proceeded to take over Lieutenant Sharpe B. as 27th Labour Group by Order ADMS 36th Divn dated 15/6/17	
"	"	2.10 pm	Capt W.S.B. HAY R.A.M.C. proceeded to Balfour on 14 days Contract-leave	
"	"	2.15 pm 6 pm	Received Warning orders to be prepared to move at short notice to MERRIS area. Arrived at English MDS Invented for immediately unpacked.	
"	"		All Wagons packed will exception of A section Wagons whose equipment was in use in Hospital	
"	17/6/17	12.30 pm half by	Received Operation Order No 33 - stating that 110th Wounded men at Bailleul who were removed to MERRIS area	
"	"	11.30 pm	Field Ambulance Operation Order No. 33	

WAR DIARY or INTELLIGENCE SUMMARY

Army Form C. 2118.

(Erase heading not required.)

Instructions regarding War Diaries and Intelligence Summaries are contained in F.S. Regs., Part II. and the Staff Manual respectively. Title Pages will be prepared in manuscript.

Place	Date	Hour	Summary of Events and Information	Remarks and references to Appendices
Bailleul	18/6/17	3 pm	Visited A.D.M.S. & received verbal instruction to detail One Officer with one Bearer sub-division to proceed to MD KLEINE VIERSTRAAT. to report to 59 F.A. to learn the line in case we should take over from them.	
		6-30 pm	Capt Bartlett with two N.C.O + 20 oth ranks proceeded to KLEINE VIERSTRAAT. + Cole Capt-Hart 109th F.A. joined them owing to a shortage of Officers in our unit - being under strength + having gone on detachment. RAMC	
		9 pm	Received O. proton Order No 3 + by ADMS 30th Div which said " that 110th F.A. should take over the premises at 16th Rue de METEREN Bailleul to 33rd F.A. 11th Div on 19th + also that 110th F.A. would take over MDS Locre + any such there from 57th F.A. and the advanced Dressing station at the Brasserie (N.16.a.1.1.), at KLEINE VIERSTRAAT. (N.10.a.9.9.) + at the LAITERIE (N.16.d.2.4) from 59th F.A. + would detail a party of one NCO + 5 men to take over walking wounded collecting station at M.24.d.2.8 from 59th F.A.	
	19/6/17	9 am	Evacuated cases to CCS + Entertained remainder to 101st F.A. (DRS)	
		11 am	Handed over Premises at 16 Rue de METEREN BAILLEUL to 33rd F.A. 11th Div	
		11.45 am	Capt C Instalec with an advance party proceeded to LOCRE to take over premises from 57th F.A.	
LOCRE	19/6/17	12-45 pm	Capt E Mercer with remainder of Units left Bailleul for LOCRE	
		2 pm	Main body of 110th F.A. arrived in LOCRE + completed finding over from 57th F.A.	
		3 pm	Visited OC 57th F.A. to arrange relief in his billet in front.	

Army Form C. 2118.

WAR DIARY
or
INTELLIGENCE SUMMARY
(Erase heading not required.)

Place	Date	Hour	Summary of Events and Information	Remarks and references to Appendices
LOCRE	19/4/17	7 pm	Visited KLEINE VIERSTRAAT. Interviewed Divisional	
		7.15 pm	Capt McD. & arranged with RC Corps Station that at	
		9.15 pm	One Bearer Sub-Division was on Officer reported for duty from 107th F.A.	
		9.50 pm	The 104th Amer: Ambulance despatched by Horse Ambulance to A.D.S KLEINE VIERSTRAAT.	
		10 pm	Proceeded to A.D.S KLEINE VIERSTRAAT. Complete handing over from 59th F.A.	
		11.30 pm	All park A.D.S. to complete, taken over from 59th F.A. + we became responsible for evacuation of line from that hour.	
	20/4/17	2 am	Arrived back from A.D.S. to HQ's after seeing patients coming through. Everything the new arrangement was working alright.	
	"	2.15 am	Reported by wire to A.D.M.S. 20th Div: that all relief was complete at 11.30 pm on 19/4/17	
	"	2.30 pm	A.D.M.S visited + inspected our M.D.S. at LOCRE + I accompanied him afterwards to A.D.S (KLEINE VIERSTRAAT) inspected + visit for duty outposts. On motor quiet for a time, got instructions from 10th F.A. of 48 Mobile Vety: Section two motor ambulances from 102nd F.A. & for attached to 110th F.A. in relief for ELSZEELE, also of A.D.M.P.	
	22/4/17	3 pm	Visited A.D.S, KLEINE VIERSTRAAT, Bonnemy + LAITERIE	
			MOR 1st R.J.R. & 9th R.J.Fus. arranged to send two Horse Ambls as usual to LAITERIE every morning to collect each of the role in support.	
	23/4/17	10 am	Was notified that Lieut cst. 4 + 6 Mobile Vet: centre with Cade patrol, had arrived to assist the	
		10.30 am	A.D.M.S arrived + inspected Capt Harts RAMC to proceed on RAET F2 to make Rec HQ the	
		11 am	Hospital + instructed Capt Honywill to take up special duties in connexion Amps ? relief	
		2.30 pm	Detached Capt. & two & to CCL Command'g. Evidence supplementary for RJCM of 2 new Received ASC attached 110th F.A.	
			Notified Capt H. on appointed to A.D.S. to relieve Capt Peake RAMC for a few hours.	

2449 Wt. W14957/Mg0 750,000 1/16 J.B.C. & A. Forms/C.2118/12.

WAR DIARY
or
INTELLIGENCE SUMMARY

Army Form C. 2118.

Place	Date	Hour	Summary of Events and Information	Remarks and references to Appendices
LOCRE	24/6/19	11 am	A.D.M.S. 39th Divn visited Hospital to get information D.B. front - we were evacuating with a draw to taking over in the near future.	
"	25/6/19	4 pm	Visited A D M S Office	
		5·30 pm	Lt Col D under O.C. returned from leave + again took over command of B the Ambulance from Capt Snowie. Snowie Capt RAMC 25/6/19	
"	25/6	6 pm	Resumed Command of 110th F.A. on return from leave.	
"	26/6/19	11 am	O.C. 49th F.A. came 15th morning to see the place we are all at.	
"	27/19	1 pm	Taking over the business and H.Q in LOCRE	
"	28/19	1 pm	Spends some hours in handing over command of the Div. Field + M.D.S. in LOCRE to 49th F.A. + moving 15 METEREN on 1st inst. Advance party of the 49th F.A. arrived at 1st taking over. Remain intermediate in charge of the [?] units up to 1st inst to watch any steps involved with the units.	
"	29/19	10 am	Visited our H.M.S. in LOCRE & 49th F.A. and writes of 15 town and two [?] officers + men of 49th F.A. had met - H.Q. Inspect the hundreds new 1st Army & such members of units known to me -	
"	"	2 pm	Proceeded to LOCRE - DRANOUTRE - METEREN.	
METEREN	"	4·30 pm	Arrived at METEREN + 12 an from our line - having proceeded	
			of 15/19 line.	

WAR DIARY
or
INTELLIGENCE SUMMARY
(Erase heading not required.)

Army Form C. 2118.

Place	Date	Hour	Summary of Events and Information	Remarks and references to Appendices
METEREN	29/6/17	3pm	Moved up to our position for 107 & 108. Batns. Reports to arrive.	
"	30/6/17	10am	Sent men on to account drift from 107 & 108 Brigades. This amount of drift coming in.	
"	"	3pm	Down to an Anzacs 31st Bn.	

18.H.Queen Street
Lt. Col Neville
O/C 110 F. Amb.

COMMITTEE FOR THE
MEDICAL HISTORY OF THE WAR
Date 10 SEP. 1917

No. 110. 7.0.

Army Form C. 2118.

WAR DIARY
or
INTELLIGENCE SUMMARY

(Erase heading not required.)

110 ⁇ Amb

Vol 2

Place	Date	Hour	Summary of Events and Information	Remarks and references to Appendices
METEREN	1/7/17	4 pm	Sentries Cpl Moir & rmen Cpl PURCE proceeding to leave	
"	2/7/17	11 am	Cpl HAY returned from leave.	
"	3/17	9 am	Returned Cpl BURTIN & rmen Cpl GLANVILLE proceeding to leave	
"	3/17	11 am	Held a Board on J/m WEEKS on C his medical classification	
"	4/17	3 pm	Dr ROUSELL held by F.G.C.M.	
"	"	6 pm	A lecture party arrived for the 1st S.A. to take over the permanent equipment in METEREN.	
"	5/17	7.31 am	Left METEREN - report attention to army and CAESTRE via & midway H.Q. & Q.S.I. L. Report & arrived Bue H.Q.	
CAESTRE	"	10 am	& Bue H.Q.	
"	6/17	5 am	Left CAESTRE Q.S.I. & arrived at RENESCURE. Report arrived L arms where H.Q	
RENESCURE	"	10.30 am		
"	7/17	4.15 am	Left RENESCURE arrived at LA WATTINE - reports trouble L Arleand J Pt MQ.	
LA WATTINE	"	11 am	Arms front & instr L. an ambulance line a bein L opening. O.R.S.	
"	8/17	4.30 pm		
"	"	10.30 am	Promoted Oriendon of L.G.C.M. Dr. James L/C DONELLY & McKay awoke the training hand to go on in K. J. L. Lunes	

2449 Wt. W14957/M90 750,000 1/16 J.B.C. & A. Forms/C.2118/12.

Army Form C. 2118.

WAR DIARY
or
INTELLIGENCE SUMMARY
(Erase heading not required.)

Instructions regarding War Diaries and Intelligence Summaries are contained in F. S. Regs., Part II. and the Staff Manual respectively. Title Pages will be prepared in manuscript.

Place	Date	Hour	Summary of Events and Information	Remarks and references to Appendices
LA WATTINES	8/2/17	11 am	[illegible] received to [illegible] the River Lens & [illegible] & [illegible] to D.T.R.S. an [illegible] in [illegible]	
		11.30 am	[illegible] to the Poste & [illegible] arose Taking - [illegible] for 15 days [illegible] onto on the troops & report to arriving 15/2 & [illegible]	
		1 pm	1 away to rise in care 15 [illegible] trip.	
	9/2/17	4 pm	Cpl EMERSON proceed on 10 days leave.	
		4.30 pm	Arrows [illegible] [illegible] - [illegible] to the [illegible] [illegible] — [illegible] w/15 DRS	
			[illegible] [illegible] [illegible] to [illegible] & [illegible] keeping horses [illegible] from 9:- P.M. in [illegible]	
	11/2/17	5 pm	Cpl BURTON [illegible]	
			[illegible] by Cpl WILSON	
	12/2/17	—	[illegible] starting for [illegible] from [illegible] [illegible]	
	13/2/17	11 am	On [illegible] had frame from [illegible] [illegible] day. Pin [illegible] [illegible]	
	14/2/17	10 am	Cpl HAY proved so never Cpl CORKEY 15- R.D.R proceeding on	
			[illegible] [illegible] [illegible]	
			[illegible] [illegible] — Our 8I.C. [illegible] — [illegible] [illegible]	
	15/2/17	4 pm	Cpl GLANVILLE [illegible] [illegible] from N.2C.7 [illegible] Group - [illegible] 15 Horses 15	
	16/2/17	4 pm	Cpl LINDSAY [illegible] from N.2C.7 [illegible] Group [illegible] [illegible] 15	
		—	ROUEN 15 [illegible] 15. Driving ltr to Reg =	
	19/2/17	—	S.M. Road [illegible] 15 [illegible] horses ([illegible] from 9 p.m.)	

WAR DIARY or INTELLIGENCE SUMMARY

Army Form C. 2118.

Place	Date	Hour	Summary of Events and Information	Remarks and references to Appendices
LA WATTINE	18/7/17	11 am	Capt. Moir reported junior from Leutpirgh Camp with Cpl N.J.R. Cpl Moir proceed to II: Lumberning Camp.	
"	19/7/17	11 am	Orders for visit to D.H.S.	
"	20/7/17	8:15 am	Sgt L. DATTINÉ with 2 orderlies. Left our escort base to return camp. Escort can convoy proceeded.	
ESQUERDES	"	11:30 am	Arrived in ESQUERDES & took over from Y.G.C.M.	
	21/7/17	2 pm	Sgt. TURNER took his 6 T.A.'s and took over in two camps.	
	"	4 pm	Party of 4 T.A.'s and N.C.O arrived in two camps. Bureau of H.M.S. & 118 F.A. in each camp in town.	
	22/7/17	3 pm	Cpl EMERSON returned from leave. Cpl CROSSIE proceed on leave.	
	23/7/17	"	Cpl EMERSON returned from leave. Cpl CROSSIE proceed on leave.	
	"	"	11: Lumbering Function. C-10 & 2.a f/c keeping duty.	
	24/7/17	10 am	Cpl BURTON proceeds to new camp 100 Rue Faidherbe.	
	"	"	Seven, 1 N.C.O. seven, to H.C. 118 A.D. trops. helping move to I.E. 118 A.A. trops.	
	25/7/17	4:15 am	Train from under Cpl EMERSON left with 107 men trops for WENNIZÉLÉ ARR.	
	"	1 pm	Cpl ESQUERDES ↑ SETROU ↑ embarking junior 7 men W/ 107 men trops for SETRUES.	

Army Form C. 2118

WAR DIARY
or
INTELLIGENCE SUMMARY
(Erase heading not required.)

Instructions regarding War Diaries and Intelligence Summaries are contained in F. S. Regs., Part II. and the Staff Manual respectively. Title Pages will be prepared in manuscript.

Place	Date	Hour	Summary of Events and Information	Remarks and references to Appendices
SETQUES	25/7/17	3 am	Embussed w/ 107 Bde front	
NENNIZEELE	"	3.30 to 7.20 pm	Capt. SETROES to WEHNIZEELE area. Arrived in billets & moved to billeting area T.8.c.4	
OUDEZEELE	26/7/17	9 am 1.15 pm	Transport arrived. Sun. Billeting party Capt GLANVILLE, 3 O.R & WATAU arr. at camp for billets.	
"	29/7/17	10 am	Lieut. & Qnr. Robinson announcing of 19.O.R. leaving 9 = 64 C.C.S. Detained Capt. GLANVILLE & CHRISTIE = party on arrival of outgoing duty in 9 = 64 C.C.S.	
"	28/7/17	10 pm	Capt BURTON returns from temp duty w/ 1/5 110 R.A.	
"	29/7/17	10 am	Capt RAWLINS reports for duty on arr. from camp.	
"	"	5 pm	Return runs to camp c/o WATAU arr. in camp	
"	30/7	8 am	Capt EMERSON w/c arr. w/ advance party & 2 lent.	
"	"	10 am	Capt CROSBIE, BURTON and RAWLINS & 3 clerks for duty on the Corps	
"	"	1 pm	Remainder (19.O.R. est) arr. in the VLAMERTINGHE Mizo.	
"	"	Evening	Wound Dressing Section in its own quarters & comm. visit cases brought in	
"	"	11 pm	Capts. OUDEZEELE for WATAU area.	
WATAU	31/7	3 am	Arrived in own quarters X24.c.9.9.	

WAR DIARY
or
INTELLIGENCE SUMMARY
(Erase heading not required.)

Army Form C. 2118

Place	Date	Hour	Summary of Events and Information	Remarks and references to Appendices
WATAU KWCQE	31/17	11 am	Capt HAY reed from Hunting Ard. dept to 1st O.S.T. detact him 15 prvts at once to return to Arends	
		9 pm	Mungo reed 15 and 1 Officer & 1 Room volunteer from S.N.A. Camp	
			fm REED FARM.	
		9 pm	Capt EMERSON proceeded to charge of Room Relations - 4 Cars arrived & went to the country. Reports 6 arrivals & that sig 37 - He thought of move That seemed convenient & that sig 37 - This travels are only employed men. I have seen in	
			Officers rep to H.Q. I am the only Officer left.	
				18 Horses Drawn
				B. CdHeene
				9c 1105 F.A

140/2224

No. 110. 7. a.

COMMITTEE FOR THE
MEDICAL HISTORY OF THE WAR
Date -1 OCT 1917

B.E.F.

SUMMARY OF MEDICAL WAR DIARIES OF 110th F.A. 36th Div.

8th Corps. 5th ARMY.

19th Corps from 26th July.

4th Corps 3rd Army from 23rd August.

Western Front Operations - July-Aug. 1917.

Officer Commanding - Lt.Col. B.H.V. DUNBAR.

Officer Commanding - Major R.G. Meredith from 15th August.

SUMMARISED UNDER THE FOLLOWING HEADINGS:-

Phase "D" 1. - Passchendaele Operations -"July-Nov.1917."

(a) - Operations commencing July 1917.

Aug. 4th,	Moves. Detachment.	1 & 2 B.S.D's to Red Farm.
6th.	"	Detachment rejoined from C.W.W.S.
7th.	Moves. To Hillhoek.	

Medical Arrangements. C.R.S. taken over from 1/2nd Wessex Field Ambulance.

8th.	Medical Arrangements.	1 T.S.D. 47th F.A. joined for duty
9th.		1 T.S.D. 108th F.A. joined for duty
15th.	Medical Arrangements.	C.R.S. handed over to Field

Ambulance of 61st Division.

Appointment. Major R.G. MEREDITH to Officer Commanding 110th F.A. vice Lt.Col. B.H.V. DUNBAR.

Moves. To Poperinghe G.11.a.4.6. Sheet 28.

17th.	Moves. Detachment.	Br. S.D's rejoined Headquarters.

B.E.F.

<u>110th F.A.   36th Div. 19th Corps.</u>   Western Front.
<u>5th ARMY.</u>   August 1917.
<u>Officer Commanding - Major R.G. Meredith.</u>
<u>4th Corps, 3rd Army from 23rd August.</u>

<u>PHASE "D" 1. - Passchendaele Operations - "July-Nov. 1917."</u>
<u>(a) - Operations commencing July 1917.</u>

<u>Headquarters at Poperinghe G.11.a.4.6.(Sheet 28.)</u>

Aug. 18th.   <u>Moves.</u> To Winnizeele J.17.a.3.4. (Sheet 27).
              <u>Moves.</u> Detachment. T.S.D. rejoined Headquarters from
              64th C.C.S.

    23rd.   <u>Moves and Transfer.</u> To 4th Corps 3rd Army and commenced
                            move to New Area.

Aug. 4th,	Moves. Detachment.	1 & 2 B.S.D's to Red Farm.
6th.	"	Detachment rejoined from C.?.?.S.
7th.	Moves. To Hillhoek.	

Medical Arrangements. C.R.S. taken over from 1/2nd Wessex Field Ambulance.

8th. Medical Arrangements. 1 T.S.D. 47th F.A. joined for du[ty]

9th. 1 T.S.D. 108th F.A. joined for d[uty]

15th. Medical Arrangements. C.R.S. handed over to Field Ambulance of 61st Division.

Appointment. Major R.G. MEREDITH to Officer Commanding 110th F.A. vice Lt.Col. B.H.V. DUNBAR.

Moves. To Poperinghe G.11.a.4.6. Sheet 28.

17th. Moves. Detachment. Br. S.D's rejoined Headquarters.

B.E.F.

3.

110th F.A.   36th Div. 19th Corps.   Western Front.
5th ARMY.   August 1917.
Officer Commanding - Major R.G. Meredith.
4th Corps, 3rd Army from 23rd August.

PHASE "D" 1. - Passchendaele Operations - "July-Nov. 1917."
(a) - Operations commencing July 1917.

Headquarters at Poperinghe G.11.a.4.6.(Sheet 28.)

Aug. 18th.   Moves. To Winnizeele J.17.a.3.4. (Sheet 27).
             Moves. Detachment. T.S.D. rejoined Headquarters from
             64th C.C.S.

23rd.   Moves and Transfer. To 4th Corps 3rd Army and commenced
                          move to New Area.

WAR DIARY
or
INTELLIGENCE SUMMARY

110 Fd Amb

(Erase heading not required.)

Army Form C. 2118

Vol 23

Instructions regarding War Diaries and Intelligence Summaries are contained in F. S. Regs., Part II. and the Staff Manual respectively. Title Pages will be prepared in manuscript.

Place	Date	Hour	Summary of Events and Information	Remarks and references to Appendices
WATAU K24.c.9.8	1/8/17	10 am	Orders received to hold 1 Bearer Subdivision in readiness to proceed to reinforce the forward clearing stations if required. Raining hard all day long.	
"	2/8/17	11 am	Line received that 1 Officer & 1 Bearer Subdivision would be retiring tomorrow at 2 pm.	
"	3/8/17	12 m	Capt EMERSON & his Bearer subdivision returned to H.Q. All the men are absolutely exhausted and their feet are in a very bad state. Some of them bleeding in French feet. Ordered them all to lie up & give their feet soak and rubbed.	
		5 pm	O.O. received for orders relative to relief of 55th Division by the 39th. I am to be prepared to take over Corps Main Station at HILL HOUSE when ordered to do so. Still raining hard.	
"	4/8/17	10 am	Weather improved today. The rain has stopped. But it is still very cloudy and windy. The men from our section, but they still require rest. They have been sent most of their equipment, but their own & the wounded. Few men have been slightly hurt & have been repaired or something.	
"		7 pm	Orders received to detail 2 Bearer Subdivisions & 1 Officer to report to MED FARM forthwith. Capt EMERSON detailed to proceed in charge of the party. M A Cars of 108 to report here & convey the party.	
		9.30 pm	Cars reported & help the party proceeded on once.	
		11 pm	Cars returned for a second journey.	
"	5/8/17	9 am	Raining day today. Rain has stopped. The sun has come out. I have in officers left here now & only about 20 NCO & men Nurse & of course all the ASC.	
"	6/8/17	3 pm	Capt EMERSON, CROSSIE & ROWLINS returned to H.Q. also the 2 Bearer Subdivisions from the Corps holding hostel Dressing Station.	

1875 Wt. W593/826 1,000,000 4/15 J.B.C. & A. A.D.S.S./Forms/C. 2118.

WAR DIARY
or
INTELLIGENCE SUMMARY

(Erase heading not required.)

Army Form C. 2118

Instructions regarding War Diaries and Intelligence Summaries are contained in F.S. Regs., Part II. and the Staff Manual respectively. Title Pages will be prepared in manuscript.

Place	Date	Hour	Summary of Events and Information	Remarks and references to Appendices
MATHS KAHEAS	6/17	7pm	*[illegible handwritten entry]*	
		8pm		
HILLHOUSE	7/17	10am	*[illegible handwritten entry]* Capt BURTON	
		11am	*[illegible handwritten entry]*	
"	8/17	9am	*[illegible handwritten entry]*	
"	9/17	9pm	*[illegible handwritten entry]*	
"	10/17	10am	*[illegible handwritten entry]* Maj. HENLE DITTY	
		11pm		
		4pm	Lt. TEWKSBURY · 2nd Lt. 100 F.A. *[illegible]*	
	11/12/17	—	*[illegible]*	
	13/17	2h	*[illegible]*	

WAR DIARY or INTELLIGENCE SUMMARY

Army Form C. 2118

Place	Date	Hour	Summary of Events and Information	Remarks and references to Appendices
HILHOEK	13/8/17	7am	to report to G.O.C. British Arriving in stores & later found	
"	14/17	"	Orders given to F.A. G.S. Div. ambs. L. Lines. This army sent to Hd. Qrs. our Dept. gents to Tine & to Cavelly of 10 F.A. Lt. Maj. MEREDITH, Major	
"	"	4pm	of TEWKSBURY reps. to 100 R.A.	
"	15/8/17	1pm	Hd. Qrs am cars. Amb. Status 1 - 2/3 R.A. 61 Rd - Ambs & IE 110 F.A. 1. Major MEREDITH hrs. 2 am arrived at 1E 110 F.A. 1. Major MEREDITH	
"	"	"	Moved 1. Ten & by hu Uplands	
				13/14 seen Duncan O.C. men
HILHOEK - POPERINHE G/11/Q 4.6	15/8/17	4pm	Took over command 110 F.A. 3 Horse Ambulance wagons sent to O.C. 108FA. RED FARM.	
"	"	8pm	F.A. proceeded here by main route, arriving 9pm.	
"	"	10pm	3 pack mules sent to PACK CAMP.	
"	"	2pm	Capt J.B Rawlin, RAMC proceeded to 12/R.I Rifles, vice Capt Dundas (wounded) [This officer was killed in action shortly after his arrival at BANK FARM.]	
"	"	4am	Capt Hay RAMC proceeded to C.H.Q.S. RED FARM. [This officer was sent from there to 13/R.I.R. vice Capt Eccles, R.A.M.C. killed in action]	
"	"	5am	Capt Burton RAMC with 36 Bearers proceeded to C.M.D.S. RED FARM. [Capt Burton proceeded from there	
"	"	8am	Capt. Emerson Cookie to O.C. C.M.D.S. RED FARM.	

R.J. Meredith, Major RAMC
G.C 100 F.A.

WAR DIARY
or
INTELLIGENCE SUMMARY.
(Erase heading not required.)

Army Form C. 2118.

Instructions regarding War Diaries and Intelligence Summaries are contained in F.S. Regs., Part II. and the Staff Manual respectively. Title pages will be prepared in manuscript.

Hour, Date, Place	Summary of Events and Information	Remarks and references to Appendices
G.11.a.6. 11.450— 16.8.17	3 large M.A Cars to Red Farm, to o.c Mob M.A.C. 5 wheeled stretchers to " " 108 F.A.	
5p.m do do	Capt Burke R.A.M.C proceeded to A.D.S. WILTJE to join 12/R.I.R.	
" 17.8.17	Capt. Emerson & Crosbie returns to duty. Capt Cocks to 45 pounds as above. 5 light litters on from 45 F.A. at J.17.2.34.	
" " "	3 Large M.A Cars 3 horse ambulances returned.	
" " "	3 horse sub division returned to duty.	
WINIZEELE J.17.a.34. 1p.m 18.8.17.	F.A annexe, braces having been transferred via M.A.C. + Horse Amb. Took over from 45 F.A. 7 collect aid from Division. Sick in Bell Tents, accommodation for 40. Main tents & bell.	
" 5p.m "	Capt Glanville R.A.M.C. + tent subdivision returned to duty from 64 CCS.	
" 7p.m 19.8.17	Lt UNGER. U.S.R reported for duty	
" 10am 20.8.17	Capt GLANVILLE to temporary duty with 10/R.I.R.	
" 10p.m 20.8.17	Capt CHRISTIE R.A.M.C returned to duty from 47 CCS.	

WAR DIARY or INTELLIGENCE SUMMARY.

(Erase heading not required.)

Army Form C. 2118.

Hour, Date, Place	Summary of Events and Information	Remarks and references to Appendices
11 a.m. 20-8-17	Capt Glanville R.A.M.C. proceeded to 10/R.I.R. for temporary duty.	
LECHELLE 9f.m 24-8-17. P31 a 5.9.	F.A. arrived having marched out from WINIZEELE at 2 a.m & entrained at ESQUELBECQUE at 8 am & reached BAPAUME at 5.30 pm. The parade were transported here in M.A. Cars.	
" 25-8-17.	Took over car from Town Major BUS. Collecting ab. from 107 Bde. Capt GLANVILLE returned to duty.	
BUS. 10 am 28-8-17. O23 d 6.4.	F.A. took over from 1/S.A.F.A. Capt DE CROSSIE & 200 O.R. took over A.D.S. at HERMIES. J29 a 5.0.	
"	Capt GLANVILLE proceeded on temporary duty with 14 R.I.R. This camp has no canteen tent & hut accommodation for 180 patients, but it is proposed to open all tents for patients also & personnel by huts. Horse & wagon standing wagons to be built.	

WAR DIARY
or
INTELLIGENCE SUMMARY.

Army Form C. 2118.

(Erase heading not required.)

Hour, Date, Place	Summary of Events and Information	Remarks and references to Appendices
BUS. 29-8-17	1/Lieut UNGER. M.O.R.C. proceeded to 48 CCS for duty.	
	Capt G.R.B PURCE & Lieut G. PHILLIPS reported for duty.	
	Submitted schemes to A.D.M.S. for billeting cont.	
" " 30-8-17		

Meredith
Lt Col RAMC
OC No F.M.

140/24 38

COMMITTEE FOR THE
MEDICAL HISTORY OF THE WAR
Date -5 NOV. 1917

No. 110 7 A.

ly # 110 3d Army Vol 24

WAR DIARY
or
INTELLIGENCE SUMMARY
(Erase heading not required.)

Army Form C. 2118.

Place	Date	Hour	Summary of Events and Information	Remarks and references to Appendices
BUS Q13.d.6.2 Sheet 57c	4/9/17	—	Capt A.W.S. CHRISTIE relieves Capt D.E. Combe at A.D.S.	
"	5/9/17	—	Capt B.R.B. PURCE 1/Lt UNGER M.O.R.C.(U.S.A) at 46 C.C.S.	
"	7/9/17	—	Capt F.J. McCARTHY reports for duty from 109 F.A. vice Lt PHILLIPS, who proceeded to 109 F.A.	
"	12/9/17	—	Capt H. EMERSON relieves Capt A.W.S. CHRISTIE at A.D.S.	
"	15/9/17	—	Capt G.W. HAWLEY, J.P. ERSKINE M.O.R.C.(U.S.A.) for 8 days instruction.	
"	17/9/17	—	Capt F.J. McCARTHY relieves Capt H. EMERSON at A.D.S.	
"	19/9/17	+US	The 2 American Officers proceeded to A.D.S. & R.A.P. & T.3.O. for instruction.	
"	20/9/17	—	Capt A.W.S. CHRISTIE assumed sanitary charge of 56 Divn Train.	
"	22/9/17	—	The 2 American Officers proceeded to 46 C.C.S. having completed their tour of instruction.	
"	26/9/17	—	Submitted list of names for Demons for New Year Leave.	
"	28/9/17	—	Capt A.W.S. CHRISTIE took over medical charge of staff of "P" Area Commandant.	
"	30/9/17	—	1/Lieut L. UNGER reports for duty from 9/R. Inns. Fus. During the past month the F.A. has been employed in collecting sick from the whole divison. Officers are collected partly by tram from the M.D.S (108 F.A.) conveying roughly

WAR DIARY
or
INTELLIGENCE SUMMARY.
(Erase heading not required.)

Army Form C. 2118.

Instructions regarding War Diaries and Intelligence Summaries are contained in F.S. Regs., Part II. and the Staff Manual respectively. Title pages will be prepared in manuscript.

Place	Date	Hour	Summary of Events and Information	Remarks and references to Appendices
			21 cases a day, partly from units in reserve, collected by its own H Ambulance, averagy 10 a day, & and call gather in from its own N.T.R. for units without M.O. averagy 8 cases a day. Cases are evacuated. (a) To Duty, roughly 5 a day. (b) To C.R.S. (1 of F.A); roughly 13 a day. These consist of cases treated in the F.A. & convalescent, or of cases passed straight thro' (unlike Scotia). By Lt Railway. (c) To C.C.S. Ordinary cases, too serious for F.A. are sent to 21 & 48 C.C.S. on alternate days by Horse Ambulance, or if severe by Cars. (d) Severe Cases are sent to various C.C.S. in accordance with IV Corps Medical Arrangements. Huts have been erected during the month, & there is now accommodation for the following cases:— Ward I. Adrian Hut 100'×22'×13'5'; floor & land outside, floored with planking inside, lighted by paraffin acetylene & warmed by 3 combustion stoves. Inlets have a grown for lining the wood with "matching" & putting glass	

WAR DIARY
or
INTELLIGENCE SUMMARY.
(Erase heading not required.)

Army Form C. 2118.

Place	Date	Hour	Summary of Events and Information	Remarks and references to Appendices
			in the ends, end altogether side windows. Porches still require to be built onto the doors. This unit takes 40 patients in beds, is used for P.U.O cases, which are segregated in Wards I & II.	
			Ward II. Similar to Ward I but not yet floored.	
			" III. Hospital Nissen Hut, takes 30 cases on stretchers & trestles, & used for ordinary medical cases.	
			Ward IV. Adrian Hut as above but not yet floored. This unit takes 54 cases on stretchers & trestles, & is used for minor surgical cases I.C.T, boils etc. This unit will be eventually floored also.	
			Ward V. 1/2 an Adrian Hut (the other 1/2 being Dr. M. Stove). takes 30 cases on stretchers & trestles, & used for classification of Probationer cases & 4	
			Ward VI. Evacuation & Racing Ward. An Adrian Hut containing a nearly dressing room & a ward for the patients' passing through.	
			When roads are being continually improved, & before winter it is hoped they will be very suitable for such cases, & serve as a refuge felt between the C.C.S.s & the various units. The total hospital accommodation is	

WAR DIARY
or
INTELLIGENCE SUMMARY.
(Erase heading not required.)

Army Form C. 2118.

Place	Date	Hour	Summary of Events and Information	Remarks and references to Appendices
			224° - There is ample room for a tented expansion to 1500 if necessary. A cook house, laundry, bath-house & drying room & chargers one built or building. In addition an Inter Hut is in use as a combined dining hall, recreation room, concert hall, & wet & dry canteen. All the above have been erected by the R.A.M.C. under the supervision of 2 Sappers R.E. The A.S.C. (M.H.T) have built car, wagon & horse standings. 16 Nissan Bow huts for the personnel are sanctioned & daily expected. Paths, roads & surface drains are being prepared. The F.A. has an A.D.S. (1 officer & 25 men) at Izy26, & sends its cases to the M.D.S. It also has 1 officer & 6 att. ambulances at 21 C.C.S.	
				Wincall RAMC Lt Col O.C. 110 F.A.

110/2499.

COMMITTEE FOR THE
MEDICAL HISTORY OF THE War
Date -8 DEC. 1917

No. 110 F.A.

Oct. 1917

40/2578

COMMITTEE FOR THE
MEDICAL HISTORY OF THE WAR
Date 17 JAN. 1918

No. 110. 7 a.

WAR DIARY or INTELLIGENCE SUMMARY

Army Form C. 2118.

110TH FIELD AMBULANCE

Place	Date	Hour	Summary of Events and Information	Remarks and references to Appendices
BUS O23 d 62 Sheet 57c	1/11/17		During the whole of last month the F.A. has remained in BUS. Work in connection with the Hospital has proceeded slowly, on account of difficulty in obtaining material. 2 Nissen Bow & 5 Vernons Huts have been erected for the personnel, but one Large Admin Hut for the remainder of the RAMCs nearly approaching the name at present very awkward into a road. The following changes took place during the month.	
			Capt N S H GAVIN RAMC. Joined from Duty 5-10-17	
			do do Posted to Nature 9-10-17	
			Charge of 14 R.I.R.	
			Capt J S H GLANVILLE RAMC Joined for Duty 9-10-17	
			from 6 R.I.R	
			1st Lt L. UNGER M.ORC U.S.A Posted to Nature 16-10-17	
			Charge of 36 Div R.E.	
			Capt F.J. McCARTHY RAMC To Nature Charge 30-10-17	
			111R Innis Fus	
			1st Lt A S ROBINSON M.O.R.C U.S.A Joined for Duty do	
			from 11 R Innis Fus	

R.J. Pruett
Lt Col RAMC
O.C. 110 F.A.

WAR DIARY or INTELLIGENCE SUMMARY

Army Form C. 2118.

110 3rd Aust...

Place	Date	Hour	Summary of Events and Information	Remarks and references to Appendices
BUS-les-Artois	14/11/17		Receive copy of Medical Arrangements 36 Divn. No S/307. 14/11/17.	
"	16/11/17		" " " 36 Divn. R.A.M.C. Operation Order No 43. 18/11/17.	
LEBUCQUIERE	17/11/17		Handed over BUS Camp to 2/L W. Ridley F.A. Headquarters & transport proceeded to LE BUCQUIERE. Capt CHRISTIE, 2 N.C.O.s & 19 men proceeded to SLAG HEAP J.34.c. to prepare walking wounded post. Capt EMERSON, 2 N.C.O.s & 18 men proceeded to A.D.S. J.29.a.5.0. Taking over from 1/Lt ROBINSON. M.O.R.C.	
"	18/11/17		Visited sites of Walking Wounded A.D.S. & R.A.P.	
J.29	19/11/17	12 am	Moved H.Q. to walking wounded Post, leaving transport, & Panniers with 8 men at L.45.80.20.5.4.0 to arrange for rations & supplies for the various parties. All motor cars parked near A.D.S.	
"	"	2 am	2 Officers, 108 O.R., 4 M.A. Cars & 6 G.S. Wagons from 109 F.D. reported for duty.	
"	"	5:30	1 Officer (Capt DAVIDSON) & 2 Bearer Subdivisions proceeded & detailed to proceed to R.A.P. K.19.b.48. at 6:30 am. 20/11/17, leaving Bearer R.A.P. J.30.b.2.7. & details	
"	"		It was to take a jumble M.O. at the R.A.P. 1 Bearer S.S.D.n (109 F.D.) in reserve	
"	"		Walking Wounded Post Established.	

Army Form C. 2118.

WAR DIARY
or
INTELLIGENCE SUMMARY
(Erase heading not required.)

Instructions regarding War Diaries and Intelligence Summaries are contained in F. S. Regs., Part II. and the Staff Manual respectively. Title Pages will be prepared in manuscript.

Place	Date	Hour	Summary of Events and Information	Remarks and references to Appendices
J29	19/4/17	10p.m	Lt ROBINSON's SB bearer established at R A P J18 b 4 2. DEMICOURT.	
"	24/4/17	6.20am	ZERO HOUR.	
"	"	11am	Wounded comg in slowly, by wheeled stretcher & hand carry from DEMICOURT & CHINESE WALL (Trip 6:45) to A D S, & walking to W W S. Probably carbs CHINESE WALL.	
"	"	2pm	Cars can cross from A D S. to loll R A P. Have obtained a MA Car from A D.N.S. from 108 F A. There is parked in a stable in HERMIES & are available cross from CHINESE WALL to A D S. 4.3 MA Cars parked at main A D S. are evacuating cases from DEMICOURT to A D S. Evacuation from A D S. by 1 MA Car from 3 109 MA Com. " W W S " 1 " 109 MA Com. & Decauville RS.	
Jigsaw	21/4/17	12a.m	W W S moved here. A D S. moved to DEMICOURT. M & DEMICOURT. DOIGNES ROAD is impassable. Therefore scheme of evacuation is as follows. In front of A D S DEMICOURT. 50 bearers 11 F A. and Lt ROBINSON, MORLE & SER'M'J'S BELL 108 F A.	

WAR DIARY
or
INTELLIGENCE SUMMARY

(Erase heading not required.)

Army Form C. 2118.

Instructions regarding War Diaries and Intelligence Summaries are contained in F. S. Regs., Part II. and the Staff Manual respectively. Title Pages will be prepared in manuscript.

Place	Date	Hour	Summary of Events and Information	Remarks and references to Appendices
Trones 0.	21/10/17 Raw (cont)		In front of R.A.P. CHINESE WALL 2 Pioneer Battalion, 109 F.A. under Capt. DAVIDSON Capt UNDER HILL R.A.M.C. Evacuates by wheeled stretcher to load carry. from A.D.S. By 4 110 M.A.Coms to W.U.S. HERMIES, thence by 109 M.A.Com A.A. 17 M.A.C. Cars via BERTINCOURT-YTRES — LEGUAVIERS. from R.A.P. CHINESE WALL by 108 M.A Com A to W.U.S. thence as for A.D.S. From W.U.S. by 109 M.A Coms to W.U.S. thence as for A.D.S.	
"	"	9p.m	Total No. of cases evacuated from 8p.m. 20th — 9p.m. 21st. 37. Officers 8p.m — 9p.m — 20th (strength 80).	
"	22/10/17 9p.m		" " 8p.m 21st — 8p.m — 22nd. 122.	
"	23/10/17 9p.m		" " 8p.m 22nd — 8p.m — 23rd 73.	
"	24/10/17 "		" " 8p.m 23rd 8p.m 24th 787.	
			During this period Lt RICHMAN, M.O.R.C. has been ready to C ADS.	

WAR DIARY
or
INTELLIGENCE SUMMARY

(Erase heading not required.)

Army Form C. 2118.

Place	Date	Hour	Summary of Events and Information	Remarks and references to Appendices
JAQAFF	24/4/4	9 p.	Capt EMERSON commands the Reserve front of A.D.S. & F.M. 2/14 has now returned to As there is insufficient accomodation at the A.D.S & R.A.P. CHINESE WALL & with road DEMICOCKS - DEIGNES is still impossable. cases must find indicates the W.S. This was found to be to congested & the father, chances adopted. Cases from A.D.S. were sent by car direct C.L.S. & & WIERE HERNIES. R.A.P. CHINESE WALL " W.W.S. as before, much as much use of tram as possable.	BRAYNE-CAMPBELL TO.
"	25/4/4	11	Capts HAYS, & 1/Lt MORGAN M.O.R.C. reported for duty. Last than 8 pm 24" — 9 pm 25". Total big Case 266.	
"	26/4/4	9 p.	" 8 pm 25" — 9 pm 26" 173.	
"	27/4/4	6 p.	Relieved by 100 F.A. & proceeded to F.A. S.C. BEAULEN COURT.	
BEAULENCOURT 24/4/4	"	"	Remained at BEAULEN COURT.	

Army Form C. 2118.

WAR DIARY
or
INTELLIGENCE SUMMARY

(Erase heading not required.)

Instructions regarding War Diaries and Intelligence Summaries are contained in F. S. Regs., Part II. and the Staff Manual respectively. Title Pages will be prepared in manuscript.

Place	Date	Hour	Summary of Events and Information	Remarks and references to Appendices
BERNAVILLE	29/9/17	9ᵃ—	F.A. (Capt Taylor) proceeded in log B.D Group, by report to BAPAUME, thence by car to RIVIERS, & thence by motor cycle home.	
COURCELLE LE-COMTE	30/9/17	1 p.m.	Transport proceeded to COURCELLE-LE-COMTE.	
"	"	5 p.	Transport arrived.	
"	"		Proceeded to COURCELLE-LE-COMTE.	
COURCELLE LE COMTE	"	11/30 a.m.	Arrived here.	

Meredith
Lt Col R.H.A.
O.C.

14/2618

COMMITTEE FOR THE
MEDICAL HISTORY OF THE WAR
Date -1 FEB. 1918

No. 110. T. O.

Army Form C. 2118.

WAR DIARY
or
INTELLIGENCE SUMMARY
(Erase heading not required.)

110 F Amb

Vol 27

Place	Date	Hour	Summary of Events and Information	Remarks and references to Appendices
BEAULENCOURT	1/11/9	9/-	Moved from COURCELLE-LE-COMTE at 1.35pm. Arrived here 6pm.	
LECHELLE	2/11/9	9/-	Proceeded for branch unit.	
MORGAN'S	4/11/9	9/-	Arrived here by march route from LECHELLE.	
		9.30	Under orders A.D.M.S. Capt CHRISTIE R.A.M.C. & 1 Lt. MORGAN M.O.R.C. & 32 beds provided & 5/14 cars to sphere O.C. 115 FA for duty with line.	
"	5/11/9	9/-	The post proceeded to METZ last night were then ordered to proceed on to RIBECOURT. All cars were delayed during the journey & are now in the	

Army Form C. 2118.

WAR DIARY
or
INTELLIGENCE SUMMARY
(Erase heading not required.)

Instructions regarding War Diaries and Intelligence Summaries are contained in F.S. Regs., Part II and the Staff Manual respectively. Title Pages will be prepared in manuscript.

Place	Date	Hour	Summary of Events and Information	Remarks and references to Appendices
MOISLANS.	5/12/17	9 A.M.	Capt CROSBIE, R.A.M.C. Capt H. HAYS, M.O.R.C. & 1 tent Subdivision forwarded to VII Corps Main Dressing Station. Finns N.A.C.O. N.A. at 11 a.m. Cpl ROBINSON & 1 man proceeded to RIBECOURT to take over a dump of artillery blankets.	
"	6/12/17	8 am noon	At 6am. 8 artillery proceeded to report to O.C. 16 F.A. 8 O.R. at METZ for duty in the lines. They were then to proceed to O.C. 17 F.A. at RIBECOURT for convoy of 108R.A & L9 31 Div. youth and ride Capt CHRISTIE. 10 O.R. incldg 2 N.C.O. proceeded at 9 a.m. under an officer 108F.D. to report O.C. 16 F.D. METZ. to form combined walking wounded post for Q 6 & 8th Div. & 49 C. Cpl ROBINSON returned from RIBECOURT, the dump of artillery not having landed onto him.	
"	8/12/17	—	5 Reinforcements arrived.	
ETRICOURT	15/12/17	6 pm.	Annie here to march route from 14016 LEANS. Parks at METZ & FINS up aware. Capt PONCE N.A.M.C. personally transferred to 48 C.C.S.	
LUCHEUX	16/12/17	10 pm.	Main Body entrained at ETRICOURT at 2 pm. arrived MONDICOURT 7.30 pm. & marched here. Transport under 1st 107 Bde transport at 8am this morning to ROCHINCOURT.	

Army Form 2118.

WAR DIARY
or
INTELLIGENCE SUMMARY
(Erase heading not required.)

Instructions regarding War Diaries and Intelligence Summaries are contained in F. S. Regs., Part II. and the Staff Manual respectively. Title Pages will be prepared in manuscript.

Place	Date	Hour	Summary of Events and Information	Remarks and references to Appendices
BEAUDRI-COURT.	17/12/17	6 p.m.	Arrived here by march route from LUCHEUX. Transport billeted by owners & parked in LE BELLEVUE. Cars billeted by owners in WARLUSEL.	
"	22/12/17		Transport repaired. Cars repaired.	
"	"			
"	23/12/17	2 p.m.	"C" Section Cars transport moved to SUS-ST-LEGER, & spend small 15 cabled hospital.	
"	24/12/17	—	Capt. H. EMERSON granted 1 month leave.	
CORBIE (LE NEUVILLE).	27/12/17	11:45 p.m.	Arrived here, having marched from BEAUDRICOURT - MONDICOURT - entrained there. S. Mjr. BELL left for leave to England.	

A.J. Annitt
Lt.Col. RAMC
O.C. 116 F.A.

COMMITTEE FOR THE
MEDICAL HISTORY OF THE WAR
Date -4 MAR 1918

No. 110. 7. O.

WAR DIARY or INTELLIGENCE SUMMARY

Army Form C. 2118.

110 3rd Army Vol 28

Place	Date	Hour	Summary of Events and Information	Remarks and references to Appendices
CORBIE.	4/1/18		Capt L.S. Glanville. R.A.M.C. posted to medical charge of 15 R.I.R.	
ROSIERS.	7/1/18		Unit arrived here by road route from CORBIE.	
BETHENCOURT.	9/1/18		" " " " ROSIERS.	
DURY.	11/1/18		" " " " BETHENCOURT.	
do.	13/1/18		Hospital accommodation for 50 cases taken over from Brench. Unit to run divisional clinic cases.	
			1/Lt. H.B. COFFMAN & A.C. BUTTON. M.O.R.C. joined for duty. A.D.S. taken over from Brench at A4.c.0.39. relay post at A5b.3.6. Sheet 66.C.	
	15/1/18		Lt. R. APPLETON. R.A.M.C. joined for duty.	
do.	21/1/18		Handed over command of 110 F.A. to Capt A.W.S. CHRISTIE. R.A.M.C.	

R.G. Marlett.

WAR DIARY
or
INTELLIGENCE SUMMARY

(Erase heading not required.)

Army Form C. 2118.

Place	Date	Hour	Summary of Events and Information	Remarks and references to Appendices
DVR	21/1/18		ADMS 36th Division inspected hospice & billets of personnel at Loothouse &c.	
do	23/1/18		DDMS 18th Corps accompanied by ADMS 36th Division inspected above hospice & made inspections.	
do	25/1/18		Capt. A.M.S. CHRISTIE visited French hospice at C.U.G.N.Y. with ADMS 36th Division & was shown the machine these carried out in connection with cases of Scarlet Fever — C.M.S. Christie	

WAR DIARY
or
INTELLIGENCE SUMMARY

Army Form C. 2118.

Place	Date	Hour	Summary of Events and Information	Remarks and references to Appendices
DoRY	27/2/18	—	CAPT DAe E. O'GRADY. R.A.M.C. reported his arrival and under instructions from Q.H.Q. took over command of the Field Ambulance from Captain A.W.S CHRISTIE. R.A.M.C. Capt H. EMERSON returned from leave. Weather fine and cold.	Telegraphy
	28/2/18	—	Captain A.W.S CHRISTIE proceed for duty at A.D.S. (A.4.C.0.3 Chat-66.C) Q.O.7.A. proceed to HAM to exploit No 153 Rue Notre Dame with a view to forming a 9 bun. with Stretcher Hand Post.	9oy
	30/2/18	—	Under instructions from A.D.M.S. I took Section Bedford Sent 15 157 Private Gene Mann to open a Corps Staron to get Later necessary equipment and 150 other ranks Corp Post from DURY were marched to the new site. Lt R. APPLETON R.A.M.C and Lt PARNELL R.A.M.C. ((G.M.R) assumed the officers detailed for this duty. Lt A.C. Button. J.S.R. left for duty at A.D.S. Heavy frost.	
	31/2/18		R.N.C.O & 10 O.R. left for C.S.D. Ham on Temporary Duty, Later the remaining Carles or Dury marched to new site. Frost.	

O'Grady Capt
MyComans
O.C. 110. Field Ambulance

CONFIDENTIAL.

WAR DIARY

OF

110th FIELD AMBULANCE.

FROM 1st FEBRUARY 1918   To 28th FEBRUARY 1918.

VOL. XXIX

WAR DIARY
or
INTELLIGENCE SUMMARY
(Erase heading not required.)

Army Form C. 2118.

Place	Date	Hour	Summary of Events and Information	Remarks and references to Appendices
DURY	1/2/18	—	O.C. visited the A.D.S. & Regimental aid posts – they lack any sort of antigas curtains or screens –	
" "	2/2/18	—	O.C. visited the Main Dyst HAM. Relay called on the D.D.M.S. with reference to Arrangements to Sain Dyst & A.D.S. to-day.	
" "	3/2/18	—	Full time parade. Infected Home lines, in the afternoon visited Skin Dyst, Ponies, and Infected Home lines.	
" "	4/2/18	—	Inspected the Sain Dyst HAM. it is not yet in satisfactory condition. Weather cloudy (fine) & showery.	
" "	6/2/18	—	Capt Christie proceeded on 14 days leave – Lt Button detailed for duty at A.D.S. O.C. visited D.D.M.S. XVIII Corps – Weather fine.	
" "	7/2/18	—	attended a Conference at D.D.M.S. office. O.C. reconnoitered forward area for a new A.D.S. hutting Sir Green in FLOQUIÈRES and F.14.D.2.4 top from the line – Sir Green attended Conference at A.D.M.S. office in the afternoon.	
" "	8/2/18	—	Inspected 5th Q⁵ Billets & Home lines. Visited Skin Dyst & Sof.	
" "	9/2/18	—	attended D.D.M.S. office – a Skin dyst in church Services has now been opened.	
" "	11/2/18	—	Visited O.D.S. & D-FLU QUERIES & arranged for an officer & fuller examination demand – Visited Infected Home 4.1	

WAR DIARY
or
INTELLIGENCE SUMMARY

Army Form C. 2118.

Place	Date	Hour	Summary of Events and Information	Remarks and references to Appendices
DURY.	13/2/18	—	ADMS visited Stan. Hospital HAM.	
	14/2/18	—	ADMS interviewed Head Q.R.S. of ambulances. Cons. with O.C.H.A. attended a conference at DDMS office with reference to medical arrangements in case of a retirement. Walks fine.	
	16/2/18	—	ADMS visited the Stan. Depot HAM. O.C. ambulances visited 2 R.E. - 9 Bns XVIII Corps. Weather friendly. Inspected Horse Lines (recent particulars will be shown) Lieut Vinton, O.C. 101 Frivate.	
	18 2/18	—	Lt. Button M.O.R.C. reported his departure for duty with the 1st R.I. Fus. Visited the ADS, 4 relay ports. Weather fine.	
	20	—	Capt. Chaplin - Dame reported from Leave. O.C.91/TA. with DDMS XVIII Corps visited the Hospital. O.C.91/TA Capt. Fullerton, R.A.M.C. reported his arrival. Vacation Lieut 9.32 of Hospital. 1.0. Officer and 11 other ranks arrived advance party from a new party.	
	21 2/18	—	A/T.A. Lieut Button Dep 1st HAM. Weather cloudy dry.	

WAR DIARY or INTELLIGENCE SUMMARY

Army Form C. 2118.

Place	Date	Hour	Summary of Events and Information	Remarks and references to Appendices
DURY	22/3	10 A.M.	The Ambulance moved off en route for "ANNOIS" under instructions from A.D.M.S. Marching party in charge of Capt. Chanter. Transport Capt. Hayes — M.O.R.C. Capt. FULLERTON R.A.M.C. reported for duty. Am Ambulance for Sick & Walking-Sick. Out of H.A.M. Weather humid & cold. Detachment A.D.S. Sheffield reported their arrival.	
	23/3		Visited the Area Commandant in Town Major. CUGNY refugees now structured attentions were Sick & wounded & sited P.W.E. site in an old German P.W.E. Weather fine.	855.
	25/3		Capt. HAYES, M.O.R.C. reported on departure from duty with no 1 General Hospital ETAPLES. Installed cellar accommodation with A.B.M.S. at ST SIMON. Then a proposed site for a nursing station.	809.
	27/3		The ADMS 36 am visits the ambulance. I recommended the Brewery Cellars at ST SIMON to arrange to leave the 95 transport for advance. 5 Wounded 1st Butterson M.O.R.C. & party. Major ditto arrived from T. Buty. — Conference of Ambulance Commanding at ABM S/4. Ambulance Commencing attack —	

ed. 0.6.16.7.H

CONFIDENTIAL

WAR DIARY

OF

110th FIELD AMBULANCE.

From 1st March 1918.   To 31st March 1918.

VOL. XXX

Lieut-Colonel,
R.A.M.C.
Commanding.

WAR DIARY
or
INTELLIGENCE SUMMARY

(Erase heading not required.)

Army Form C. 2118

Instructions regarding War Diaries and Intelligence Summaries are contained in F.S. Regs., Part II. and the Staff Manual respectively. Title Pages will be prepared in manuscript.

Place	Date	Hour	Summary of Events and Information	Remarks and references to Appendices
ANNOIS	1.3.18	—	Visited the Stretcher Bearers H.A.M. with reference to Sanitary Arrangements - weather fine -	softly
	2.3.18	—	Visited the A.D.M.S. office re medical arrangements - in the afternoon held a gas parade, all ranks, granted 8 days leave in France - Handed over to Capt. Christie - came t.o.c. -	softly
	5.3.18	—	Lieut. + Q.M. PARNELL went on 14 days leave to England.	softly
	6.3.18	—	Reported my return from leave; Inspected Ambulance Site + Horselines - weather fine -	softly
	8.3.18	—	Visited the A.D.M.S. office reference Ambulance detail. Also visited the proposed Remain station at S. SIMON.	softly
	10.3.18	—	In the morning I visited Stretcher Bearer H.A.M. Afternoon had an alarm gas parade without warning - this was carried out + the men continued their work for 15 minutes wearing respirators. Held a fire drill parade at 11 A.M. Inspected Horse lines etc - satisfactory weather fine	softly
	11.3.18	—	The XVIII Corps Night the Ambulance reference cars -	softly
	13.3.18	—	The A.D.M.S. + D.D.M.S. XVIII Corps + D.D.V.S. inspected the Horses. satisfactory. Accommodation.	softly
	15.3.18	—	The XVIII Corps Horse master visited the ambulance + inspected the Horse transport - satisfactory - gave no medical arrangements -	softly
	19.3.18	—	Visited the A.D.M.S. office re accommodation for 150 Stretcher Bearers + 200 to 300 Walking Wounded + also cellars	softly

weather fine

WAR DIARY
or
INTELLIGENCE SUMMARY
(Erase heading not required.)

Army Form C. 2118

Place	Date	Hour	Summary of Events and Information	Remarks and references to Appendices
ANNOIS.	20/3/18	—	In the morning held a firm drill & gas parade. at 2.30.P.M. I received orders to reconnoitre the villages of CUGNY and BROUCHY for suitable sites for Dressing Stations. on arrival at CUGNY the avenue at every accommodation for Stretcher and walking cases. — Billet not broncher was found a suitable place with clear accommodation for 200 to 300 cases. Officers mess & Orderly Room — upstairs, accommodation for 200 to 300 cases. Apparent rooms & rooms. Lt- A.D.M.S at 7. P.M. — Weather foggy & damp.	Coy.
ANNOIS.	21/3/18	6.30 A.M.	Received a dispatch from A.D.M.S — "MAN BATTLE POSITIONS". on which I immediately carried out previous arrangements. — 30 Bearers under Capt. ANDERSON — R.A.M.C.(T). were despatched in his Motor ambulance to Le HAMEL where the opened a Dressing Station in Huts by the bridge head. — The remainder of the ambulance moved to St SIMON, arriving at 8.15. A.M. & immediately opened a Dressing Station & prepared for the reception of Stretcher cases and walking wounded. Capt. FULLERTON - M.C. R.A.M.C reported his arrival at 11.45. A.M. Capt. EMERSON.M.C. " " " a little later. —	
St SIMON	21/3/18	8.30 A.M.		
	12.— Noon	AT. Noon. the A.D.M.S gave me orders to reconnoitre an alt- site as the A.D.S at- Qn. SERACOURT had ceased its function on account of Shell fire and the rapid advance of the German Infantry. 1st of Enemy arrived at- 12.15. P.M. Evacuation of wounded carried out- in 2 circuits forward of the A.D.S St SIMON by Sections the 2/1st. M.A.C.	

WAR DIARY or INTELLIGENCE SUMMARY

Army Form C. 2118

Place	Date	Hour	Summary of Events and Information	Remarks and references to Appendices
ANNOIS	21/3/18		From noon onwards the wounded came in considerable numbers, principally walking cases. The site of A.D.S. proved very satisfactory & of sufficient accommodation. The D.D.M.S. XVIII Corps visited the A.D.S. during the afternoon. The German's intense bombing H.E. Shrapnel continually during the day over "St Simon" bridge head and downwards even the A.D.S. & village causing many casualties amongst the artillery & transport. The A.D.M.S. visited the A.D.S. in afternoon & ordered is report to A.D.M.S. officer at "OLLEZY" where 1 received orders to evacuate the A.D.S. by midnight as the bridges over the Canal were to be blown up.	
		10.30 P.M.	All patients, stores etc. were for BROUCHY. The patients arrived at O.D.S since 11.15 P.M. 1.15 A.M. that the Germans were advancing rapidly. Reports say that Capt. Anderson returned from A.B.S. Le HAMEL at 4 P.M. without any orders from me. He was sent back with 2 Ambulance cars to collect stragglers - this he did continually until 11 P.M. picking up numbers of cases on the road. The Ambulance trains for- meanwhile had moved from A.D.M.S. Wilt O.C. 109" F.A. A.D.S.S. to BROUCHY. 12 officers & 359 O.R.s No of cases passed through A.D.S. was reported capture of Dr MINNEGAN RT, Wilt Fd Amb No.21 & H/c LILLEY - Wd. Killed 3r Williams in W----	

WAR DIARY or INTELLIGENCE SUMMARY

Army Form C. 2118

Place	Date	Hour	Summary of Events and Information	Remarks and references to Appendices
BROUCHY	22/3/18	6 A.M.	We arrived at "Brouchy" at 6 A.M. occupying No I. Billet with 109th F.A. The news of the Battle is not satisfactory, our troops slowly retiring, fighting a rearguard action. German troops are reported to be on our Divisional left flank.	
		12.30 P.M.	The Ambulance received orders from A.D.M.S. to proceed along to ESMERY-HALLON and billet out at 1. P.M. Capt. EMERSON being sent forward as billeting officer.	
		1.30 P.M.	Arrived at ESMERY-HALLON at 4.30 P.M. no billets to be found so I moved on about 2 kilometres & billeted at HOSPITAL FARM. I met the A.D.M.S. at 6. P.M. and received instructions to return to "BROUCHY" then go open an A.D.S. I started with 40 bearers & 4 officers at 6. P.M. and arranged a dressing station in the ruined chateau – there is plenty of shelter had the Cellar accommodation is very limited. at 8.30. P.M. I visited the H.Q of 108th & 109th Brigades informing the G.O.C's of the arrangements made. The Line we are to clear is that between OLLEZY on the left and SUMET on the right. At the Somme Lines Revd. Capt. FULLERTON + ANDERSON came forward with an Ambulance to get in touch with the R.M.O's and Battalion Commanders. They returned at 11.30 A.M. having found arrangements as Whole Were	
		8.30 P.M.		

WAR DIARY or INTELLIGENCE SUMMARY

Army Form C. 2118

Place	Date	Hour	Summary of Events and Information	Remarks and references to Appendices
BROUEHY	22/3/18	11.30 PM	The Divisional Front lying along the "SOMME CANAL" between SOMMETTE - EAUCOURT and "OLLEZY". R.A.P's were found in the railway cutting at the former & near the bridge head in the latter place - All wounded were directed to these points where an advanced Div. Coll. of Capt. FOLLERTON - Division Ambulance Cars collected them & evacuated to the Dressing Station at "BROUEHY" - there many derived wounds and dispatched in Ambulance Cars to C.C.S - A considerable number of cases collected during the night at No. A.C. Cars did not arrive as arranged - Lieut dispatched motors to 10th & 104th T. A. for all their available Cars - these arrived next day - No. of Cases passed through 33. O.R. Weather damp & windy & foggy -	
BROUEHY	23/3/18	7.30 AM	Cases have continued to come in pretty rapidly & there was a difficulty owing to shortage of M.A.C. Cars. 3 similar cars got back at 8. A.M. from C.C.S. these were immediately sent on to the forward area. Many more Ambulances (mag wag.) Corpl. Ward - M.T. had up to this time evacuated the front line. Single handed.	
	10 AM	The General has commenced shelling & several H.V. shorts full their burst near the Dressing Station - nobody however was injured - the A.D.M.S visited the A.D.S. at 1.P.15. M.T. found the transport lines unsuitable as holders	

WAR DIARY
or
INTELLIGENCE SUMMARY
(Erase heading not required.)

Army Form C. 2118

Place	Date	Hour	Summary of Events and Information	Remarks and references to Appendices
BRODENY	23/3/18		Towing to a Stn. between HRETOY la Valens and BEAULIEU - sat down in farm des FONDS GAMETS when they parked 108th F.A. 109th F.A. being in a field close by.	
" "	" "	12.30 P.M.	Had a wild & Bromley Bluff - Continued traversos with Brigades Hd. Q'rs. by means of having a dispatch rider at Hd. Q'rs. who reported demands to me - I visited Hd. Q'rs. 2 several times that the Brigade was moving back and met the Hd. Q'rs. advance upon at "BERLANCOURT". I sent the trick and men on to VILLESELVE remaining with 3 bearers & south of Roma - to bear the last lot of patients. Capt. HILLERTON & Capt. EMERSON to dear the last lot of patients. Capt. HILLERTON will 3 Cars was then brought to VILLESELVE taken on by transport. A.D.S. was pushed at BERLANCOURT. The A. Buns.	
BERLANCOURT	23/3/18	3. P.M.	and S.B. both leaves during the afternoon. Very few cases were coming down.- Capt. HILLERTON continued his Car service during the afternoon. Several M.A.C. Cars arrived and the Evacuation went on without a halt. Here again a double system of Car evacuations was formed - one system to VILLESELVE and the other to find outside GOLANCOURT. Both evacuating to the Collecting Post at BERLANCOURT. 2. M.O. were posted on each system - I proceeded at 8.30 P.M to the relieves at TIRLANCOURT with duty & 1 mud. officer to help with our divisional wounded - O.C. 111th F.A. 141st division who was running the greatest Stationary Cases passed through 96, O.R. officers 2 Lts. Weather foggy & damp.-	

Army Form C. 2118

WAR DIARY
or
INTELLIGENCE SUMMARY
(Erase heading not required.)

Instructions regarding War Diaries and Intelligence Summaries are contained in F.S. Regs., Part II and the Staff Manual respectively. Title Pages will be prepared in manuscript.

Place	Date	Hour	Summary of Events and Information	Remarks and references to Appendices
BERLANCOURT	24/3/18	8 A.M.	Visited Capt. Fullerton at Villeselve and Dr Coffman at Golancourt. They had very little work during the night - our cases are being passed through the Graafs of 44th F.A. at 10 A.M. Lt Osborne visited the RAP's and the Chateau - 10.30 A.M. orders obtained to load our RAP's and proceed to wounded to 109th F.A. finish evacuation to 109th F.A. - finish evacuation to both officers in charge of Coy Systems to show the ambulance officers the Roisels and Annexits at Authancourt on being relieved - ordered O.O.-109/4 Villeselve and Golancourt system 2 - the Germans have commenced shelling Villeselve and the Chateau TIRANCOURT. WSH. handed over to O.O. 109 F.A.	v/88/2 - 1
		2 P.M.	Left for the Chateau TIRANCOURT. WSH. handed over to O.O. 109 F.A.	
		3 P.M.	Received orders to move to AMY when we arrived at 6 P.M. - a few sick were collected on Route and brought down with the transport - Capt's Christie & Fullerton arrived at 9.30 P.M. with all detailed units from an Ambulance - Weather 40994.	
AMY -	24/3/18	6 P.M.	Some 60 to 80 cases were passed through books of 114th F.A. from during our own RCY	
WARSY	25/3/18	9 A.M.	The Ambulance moved off under orders from ADMS to WARSY where billets, and marked self.	
		2.30 P.M.	we arrived at 2.30 P.M. The Unit	
WARSY GRIVESNES	26/3/18	1 P.M.	Received orders to move to "GRIVESNES" where we arrived at 3.45	
		6 P.M.	Unit moved into Billets H.ABS. visited the transport - Weather foggy.	8.09

WAR DIARY
or
INTELLIGENCE SUMMARY
(Erase heading not required.)

Army Form C. 2118.

Hour, Date, Place	Summary of Events and Information	Remarks and references to Appendices
GRIEVESNES 27/3/18 10:30 A.M.	Received orders from O.D. Div 2. to move to AUBVILLERS.	
AUBVILLERS. 12. NOON.	Arrived at noon in company with 105 & 109 F.A.3. found billets for the men – ABRIS. visited the Ambulance & ordered us to proceed to CHIRMONT.	
1.30 " " 4 P.M.	The Ambulance moved off at 6.15 P.M. arriving at	
CHIRMONT. 11.30 P.M.	CHIRMONT at 11.10 P.M. when the Unit billeted.	Pigs.
	with Poilus & civils	
CHIRMONT 28/3/18 6.30 AM	Received orders to proceed to LAWARDE where	
	we arrived at 10.30. A.M. Capt EMMERSON going forward	
	as billeting officer.	
LAWARDE 14.30.	The A.D.M.S arrived at 4.30 P.M. and instructed me	
	to open an A.D.S at LA FALOISE as the Division will	
	again in the Line – in Reserve to the 2 rud.	
" " 6 P.M.	I proceeded to LA FALOISE with Capt. FULLERTON &	
	Rev Major Hollaran to arrange a site for A.D.S	
	Cars started to get in touch with the Brigades	
LA FALOISE. 7.15 P.M	arrived at LA FALOISE when we reported the G.O.C.	
	time for A.D.S. Also saw the Brigadier.	
	Cars stands were settled at "BOULLEMALLE" & "ESCLAINVILLIERS"	
	Bar. Fullerton got in touch with the R.M.O. of the Brigade	

WAR DIARY or INTELLIGENCE SUMMARY.

(Erase heading not required.)

Army Form C. 2118.

Instructions regarding War Diaries and Intelligence Summaries are contained in F. S. Regs., Part II. and the Staff Manual respectively. Title pages will be prepared in manuscript.

Hour, Date, Place	Summary of Events and Information	Remarks and references to Appendices
LA FALOISE - 28th 11.P.M.	Knigadeil one in Billets and the germans reported to have flung back 6 to 8 kilometres by the french. The A.D.M.S. visited the A.D.S's during the evening.	
LA FALOISE, 29th 9.A.M.	Nothing disturbed the night - I visited the Car parks at 7.30.A.M. The ammunition had no fighting - a few Sick & accidental wounds were attended to. I visited the Transport lines and arranged for the Evacuation of Capt EMERSON 15 C.C.S suffering from Parrolliti - The A.D.M.S. visited the A.D.S, a few Stands at 11.30 P.M.	
" " " 3.30.PM	Received orders to close A.D.S & Major H. Renfords at LAWARDE. arrived at 5-30.P.M.	
5.30.PM	Received orders to proceed to "NAMPS au VAL" the A.D.M.S told me that the Division is being withdrawn from the line.	
6.30.P.M.	Left - La Faloise with the 108 + 109- F.A. The were a very fatiguing march on the road many flares was flashed whilst timed infantry Battalion whom were had to march. The last mile was very bad hill	

Army Form C. 2118.

WAR DIARY
or
INTELLIGENCE SUMMARY.
(Erase heading not required.)

Instructions regarding War Diaries and Intelligence Summaries are contained in F.S. Regs., Part II. and the Staff Manual respectively. Title pages will be prepared in manuscript.

Hour, Date, Place	Summary of Events and Information	Remarks and references to Appendices
WAILLY 29/3/18 11.45 P.M.	I met the O. bme who informed me that our billeting area in the next village 5 miles - (NAMPS au VAL) I contacted the owner and learned from the village maire Café Etinkie, our billeting officer who informed me that there was no billets to be had. Therefore decided 25 yards on the roadside to the remainder of the night. Weather very cold and	
(M)ile from - NAMPS au VAL 30/3/18. 2.45 AM.	Some Rain.	
" " 10. A.M.	The men marched to billets in NAMPS au VAL at 12.30. the O Bnd visited the Ambulance station that morning. Pats arrived. Orders received for the Bn to march out of SALEAU. Sent Transport. Transport of all three F.A's moved off at 6.30 P.M. March to LONG ROY-GAMACHES.	Digby
7.30 P.M.	Personelle marched to SALEUX Railhead to Entrain for the same destination. Horse lines detailed to leave this evening the rear and billets. Bns set off tomorrow morning. Weather warm	Digby

(73989) W4141—463. 400,000. 9/14. H.&J.Ltd. Forms/C. 2118/10.

WAR DIARY
or
INTELLIGENCE SUMMARY
(Erase heading not required.)

Army Form C. 2118

Place	Date	Hour	Summary of Events and Information	Remarks and references to Appendices
SALEUX.	3/1	9.AM.	The T.A.S personnel are still awaiting a train - there were heavy rain during the night - and no shelter available. Moved off with the Motor Convoy at 8.30. AM arriving at our Billeting Village at 1.15. P.M. I put the 2 Bn'd at railhead who kill me that the personnel had not yet started.	
COURTEUX	1"	6.30 P.M.	The Transport arrived at Billets (Courteux) no word of personnel. So I sent an officer with a Car to await their arrival at rail head - weather fine -	Biography.

Secret

War Diary

of

110th Field Ambulance

From 1st April 1918   To 30th April 1918.

Volume XXXI

Army Form C. 2118.

WAR DIARY
of
INTELLIGENCE SUMMARY.
(Erase heading not required.)

Instructions regarding War Diaries and Intelligence Summaries are contained in F.S. Regs., Part II. and the Staff Manual respectively. Title pages will be prepared in manuscript.

Hour, Date, Place	Summary of Events and Information	Remarks and references to Appendices
1st APRIL, 1918. COURTIEUX.	Capt CHRISTIE with remainder of personnel arrived at HdQrs having entrained at SALZUX at 3 A.M. The entraining was 36 hours late. Unable to obtain in transit a suitable billet for a detention Hospital the H. fixed on an empty farm in VISSE, made arrangements to move Hospital Staff this afternoon. A.D.M.S. visited the unit + informed him that we went to entrain again tomorrow. Weather fine.	Geography. Boe.
2-4-18. COURTIEUX.	The morning and afternoon were spent rearranging the Baggage, Waggons + cleaning up, waiting for (Capt. ANDERSON - R.A.M.C. reported his departure for 16. R.I.R.	Boe.
3. 4. 18. FOURTIEUX.	Packed Baggage and received orders from A.D.M.S. to entrain from FEUQUIERES for PROVEN. Time. Transport to entrain at 3. A.M. 4. inst. " " " " 6. A.M. " " Personnel " " " " " " Motor Transport to proceed by road under Capt. CHRISTIE rendez-vous for 3. 4. A- at FEUQUIERES at 9 A.M. Weather showery.	Boe
4. 4. 18. COURTIEUX. FOUQUIERES.	Little at times. Arrived at rail head as above - Commenced entraining at 6.30 A.M. - completed at 10 A.M. without incident + train started 10.15.	

(73989) W4141—463. 400,000. 9/14. H.&J.Ltd. Forms/C. 2118/10.

Army Form C. 2118.

WAR DIARY
or
INTELLIGENCE SUMMARY.
(Erase heading not required.)

Instructions regarding War Diaries and Intelligence Summaries are contained in F. S. Regs., Part II. and the Staff Manual respectively. Title pages will be prepared in manuscript.

Hour, Date, Place	Summary of Events and Information	Remarks and references to Appendices
4.4.18.	Nothing of moment occurred during the journey which was via:- ABBEVILLE - Calais, BERG - PROVEN. Weather fine. Journey is Wet & Rain with nightfall.	Bogrady.
5-4-18. PROVEN.	Detrained at 2 A.M. in a Rainstorm. Personnel proceeded by Lorry - divisional Hospital Farm Camp, A.D.M.S. visited camp at 12. noon + later orders to move to L'EBBE FARM GWALIOR FARM + L'EBBE in the afternoon + 33rd div M.I Q-- in the evening - fine weather.	
HOSPITAL FARM CAMP.		bugs.
6.4.18.	LIEUT. COFFEMAN. U.S.R. reports for duty for the 12th- M.I.R. Unit paraded at 9.45 A.M. moved off at 10. A.M. arriving L'EBBE FARM at 12. noon, took over the Hospital (11th Corps + Stain P. [?]) from a detachment of the 141 F.A. found many gas shelling across the road, the old 18th Corps outfit Vet-Sect Site - men accommodation in stream huts - new horse lines - vaccination finished -	Pat.
L'EBBE FARM 12. noon.		
7.4.18. L'EBBE FARM.	Retired Personnel - Unpacked Waggons + made General inspection of new site. 4 Bruil visited the Fourfiled durings the day - fine weather.	Body.

(73989) W4141—463. 400,000. 9/14. H.&J.Ltd. Forms/C. 2118/10.

WAR DIARY
or
INTELLIGENCE SUMMARY.
(Erase heading not required.)

Army Form C. 2118.

Hour, Date, Place	Summary of Events and Information	Remarks and references to Appendices
8. 4-18. LIBBRE FARM.	10 A.M. – transferred transport arranged station fire pickets, alarms etc., we took over 44 section loan with be impressed. B/Capt. 11th Corps Col. Thom. A.M.S. visited us in the afternoon. Weather fine - cold.	B/S
9. 4. 18.	Had six infection by Sections - Section Commanders to take all tents of deficiencies in by 2. P.M. 10 unit completed with Equipment from Rubbish eaten fire.	fine.
10. 4. 18.	Rained. 11th Corps visited the Hospital. In the afternoon the Ambulance played the Coys of Staff at - Football - a win 2, 5 + 1, a failure. There was an scrambling the wards today partly weather cold a drizzle.	fog.
11. 4. 18.	Inspection of gas respirators. 2. P.M. Orders issued that all equipment - mob stores shall be checked by Sections.	

Capt. L.W. JESSAMAN M.O.R.C. reported their arrival 1/Lt F.E. MILLER O.S.R. for duty.
A.Girish visited the Ambulance Watts Capt. Culy

WAR DIARY
or
INTELLIGENCE SUMMARY.
(Erase heading not required.)

Army Form C. 2118.

Hour, Date, Place	Summary of Events and Information	Remarks and references to Appendices
L'EBBE FARM 12.4.18.	Inspected Horse Lines – M.T. + personnel Huts. In afternoon held FIRE DRILL + inspected Hospital. Weather fine – the D.D.M.S. II corps visited ambulance	POD
13.4.18.	Administration at 10 a.m. Funeral at 2 p.m. of an orderly officer – Watts – The A.D.M.S. visited the unit.	PODG
14.4.18.	Church parade 6 P.M. Weather fine but cool –	Jog
15.4.18.	Inspection L.M. orders at 10 a.m. The Unit was paid at 2 p.m. – The a Brig. visited the Unit in afternoon.	Jog
16.4.18.	A visit to BBY Camp in view of orders that we may to the it. over. this is now in a Corps Counsellor Station. Walked visited the Camp. Weather cold. Damp.	Jog

WAR DIARY
or
INTELLIGENCE SUMMARY.
(Erase heading not required.)

Army Form C. 2118.

Hour, Date, Place	Summary of Events and Information	Remarks and references to Appendices
L'EBBE FARM 14.4.18	D.D.M.S. 2nd Corps visited the hospital. Huns shins + sides - In the afternoon the A.D.M.S. inspected the hospital. Several cases were infected by Sisters & etc - "Gas" Instruction by Sisters & gas parade.	
18.4.18	Capt Christie & Capt Jarreman, M.O.R.C. left for Tubby Camp to take over 2nd Corps Rest Depôt - with 2.0 - O.R. (near Rousz-Brugges) All equipment supplies & mob details - 200 Stretchers too lately sent to 106 H.A. at PROVEN. At Bus-vinidal this unit.	
19.4.18	The Unit in areas complete on tour on equipment in convenant - Canteria Mob. Equipment has not yet arrived. Luck away that it has been indented for. The Germans are shelling the area with H.V. Guns and our Aëroplanes dropped a qued aërial torpedo on Huns lines at 10.30-PM - no damage - Weather fine.	

Army Form C. 2118.

WAR DIARY
or
INTELLIGENCE SUMMARY.
(Erase heading not required.)

Instructions regarding War Diaries and Intelligence Summaries are contained in F.S. Regs., Part II. and the Staff Manual respectively. Title pages will be prepared in manuscript.

Hour, Date, Place	Summary of Events and Information	Remarks and references to Appendices
20.4.18. L'EBBE FARM	Divided coys Con Camp. with Major Emerson informed. Visited the Camp. Saw 4 visited ORs & OCs in Con Camp. — The Germans dropped 6 bombs near the farm last night. Weather fine —	OSS.
21.4.18. " " "	Church Parade C.E. — 4 P.M. Rolicris — 5 P.M. Pres. — 3 P.M. Weather fine —	Oss.
22.4.18. " " "	Inspected Hospital & Sandmere — fatigue parties working on Barrel Specific Shelters. Scout party this morning. OCW 11th Parnall medical Cofer Em Gebt. visit inoculated T.A.B. Weather fine —	Oss.
23.4.18. " " "	Inspected Home Divn. Hospital. In the afternoon The A.D.M.S visited the Ambulance reference to starting a school for the American officers to join. duration of 6 days, duration weather fine —	Oss.

WAR DIARY
or
INTELLIGENCE SUMMARY.
(Erase heading not required.)

Army Form C. 2118.

Hour, Date, Place	Summary of Events and Information	Remarks and references to Appendices
L'EBBE FARM. 24.4.18.-	J Rd to hotspur. The further inspection of the area in 10% of the 1st Res. and many M.T. here. a malaise. some cases vomiting - reported to Hospital.	Very dry.
" " " 25.4.18.-	very heavy shelling to the N.E. of YPRES & many enemy planes came over bombing. Enemy painting waggons. Weather fine. rain storm in evening.	Dry.
" " " 26.4.18	Juspects to Hospital. Horse lines - Reviewed running and medical arrangements. Strike come sick ponies in the armies of the Enemy attacking our strong second front. Staff Conference at A.D.M.S. office 6.P.M.	Weather windy.
27.4.18.- L'EBBE FARM	Orders received to move to TUBBY Camp (Rouge trooper) granted at 10.30. A.M. - after handing over to the 139 F.A. (41 Div.). 16 sick patients sent by Ambulance car's immediately marched - Arrived TUBBY Camp at 1.15 P.M. Main depot opened also 36 divisional Rest Station and remainder of Corps Con Depot while still has 132 patients in.	
" " " " TUBBY. CAMP. 1.30. P.M.	Arranged Bultin allotting available huts etc - CAPT. FULLERTON reported his arrival from 109 F.A. Weather cold + chilly. Inspection of Buildings. Arranging sorting of patients. Detailing details. Site - 2 trainloads of material arrived	
28.4.18. -	from 109 F.A. - The D.D.M.S. 11th Corps visited - Conf: win it-2 re Hospital Arrangements + Rationing - Enemy - Hot Weather Showers	Dry.

WAR DIARY or INTELLIGENCE SUMMARY

Army Form C. 2118.

Hour, Date, Place	Summary of Events and Information	Remarks and references to Appendices
29-4-18 TUBBY CAMP.	Visited the 2nd Corps Hd. Qrs re medical arrangements and evacuations. The A.D.M.S. visited the Convoy & dismissed the Companys. Held Med. Board on a man for Base Dup 27 - Heavy Heavy gun fire to S.E. our KEMMEL divisions where the enemy are attacking. Capt JESSEMAN - M.O.R.C. reported his departure for ABBEVILLE under Shrmes - Col. P.B.	
30.4.18.	I visited Railhead PROVEN - Rousse Brauges & CROMBEEK reference return of men fit for duty to their units. the Corps Convalescent Depôt in now closed & all patients cleared either to D.R.S -, C.C.S or to duty. Held a Concert for Patients in afternoon - weather dull & cold -	photography

Secret

May 1918

War Diary of
110th Field Ambulance

May 1918   Volume XXXII

No. 32

WAR DIARY or INTELLIGENCE SUMMARY

Army Form C. 2118

(Erase heading not required.)

Place	Date MAY	Hour	Summary of Events and Information	Remarks and references to Appendices
TUBBY CAMP. W.19.d.6.7. 51st 19 Bdgms Tabunc	1 5/18	—	Infants Hospital grounds – Shain Dupot. Horse Lines, etc. The A.D.M.S visited the Camp. opened a round for officers arranged for supply of fuel milk visits the Area Commandant. Weather dull & cold.	before dry
" "	2nd	—	The A.D.M.S visited the Camp. Held "Fire alarm" at 2 P.M. Inspected Horse Lines – Weather warm –	"
" "	3rd	—	The D.D.M.S Inspected the Camp – Shein Dupot – made Suggestions as various Mess House. Wards etc. The A.D.M.S called before – Weather fine, warm – Germans dropped 12 shells near Railway 200 yds from Camp – 1 Horse Wounded –	B.G.S.
" "	4th	—	I attended Conference at A.D.M.S office afternoon medical arrangements in the event of a new grand action – the Corps are starting a C.M.D.S – D.A.D.M.S – M.T. A.S.C is ahead the M.M Divis Rouls Brg). Divis standby M.T. A.S.C is ahead the M.M for brownes with recent Questions near ST QUINTIN. Weather fine.	B.G.S.
" "	5th	—	Church Parade Pres. 10.15 – C of E 11.30 – R.C: 9.30 & 10.30 A.M. The A.D.M.S & D.A.D.M.S attended Church Service & Inspected the Camp also held P.B. Board on some patients – Weather thunder showers	B.G.S.
" "	6th	—	Fire drill at 11 A.M. Inspected Infected –	B.G.S.
" "	7th	—	The D.D.M.S – 2nd Corps visited the Hospital. Very Heavy gun fire Capt. O.V. Burrows – M.C R.A.M.C reported fire – gratful firing – arrived for duty	B.G.S.

WAR DIARY
or
INTELLIGENCE SUMMARY
(Erase heading not required.)

Army Form C. 2118

Place	Date	Hour	Summary of Events and Information	Remarks and references to Appendices
TUBBY CAMP. W.17.d.6.7.	MAY 8	-	The D.D.M.S - 11th Army with D.D.M.S 11th Corps visited the arrangements - He was pleased with the arrangements - Capt Parry, in attached to the Dental Surgeon from 36 B.C.C. 25 San Sect. United the Camp refreshments Soldiers Kits Unit for 4 days a locker to be added. Very heavy gun fire all night - weather very fine	topog[raphy]
	9	-	Started physical drill for personnel & convalescent patients - 3/4 hour for patients morning & evening - Inspected Hospital & Horse Lines. very fine & warm - Capt Gimblett - Wesleyan Chaplain reported arrived - opened ward for Scotia officers - weather fine	86.
	11	-		fine
	12	-	Church Parade - The Tobin disinfector arrived for 1 day all the Unit at work cleaning etc. weather - Capt J MORHAM, R.A.M.C.T. reported his arrival for duty.	'51
	13	-	2nd Corps Visited Camp & Inspected wards offices etc. also the A.D.M.S 36 Division arrived - Held Medical Board on men for Boots Bapst also Inspected Hospital - weather warm	'51
	14	-	A.D. M.S 33rd Division visited the Camp - I visited the 101st F.A. reference medical arrangements. weather warm - fine	J.77.
	15	-	Inspected Camp + Horse Lines - Paid the Unit Walking	fine
	16	-	Camp + Horse Lines inspected by Major Gen. Coffin - V.C. D.S.O. Divisional Commander - who said the place was good -	'51

WAR DIARY
or
INTELLIGENCE SUMMARY

Army Form C. 2118

(Erase heading not required.)

Place	Date	Hour	Summary of Events and Information	Remarks and references to Appendices
Tilly (camp sheet 19. W.27.d.6.7.)	19/5/16	-	A.D.M.S. visited the Hospital, inspected all the Cases more especially the P.U.O.'s. Inspected Horse Lines & Skin depôt. weather very hot.	DDY
	19/5/16	-	Inspected Hospital & Horse Lines. Weather fine -	DDY
		-	Church Parade - C.of E. Pres. & R.C. -	
	20/5/16	-	D.D. Md 2nd Corps visited the Camp and arranged for the extension of the Skin depôt to 150 Beds. weather very hot - Capt. Appleton departed on leave dated 21st inst -	DDY
	21/5/16	-	A.D.M.S visited the Hospital, made investigations into the breaking of the Band of the Division. played from 4 - 6 . P.M. weather very hot -	DDY
	22/5/16	-	Held a Fine alarm at 11. A.M. fine picket turned out. I think weather very hot -	DDY
	23/5/16	-	A.D.M.S visited the Hospital Rest Burial + to Bee Brigot - Inspected the wards. weather v. hot -	DDY
	25/5/16	-	Start inoculating the Horse Wise bull for Scabies - The Second Corps. is now in India supply.	DDY
	26/5/16	-	The O. Brig. 11th Corps visited the Hospital, medical arrangements & inspected the Horse Lines which we have to share with some French D.O.T. troops. weather fine - east.	DDY

WAR DIARY
or
~~INTELLIGENCE SUMMARY~~

(Erase heading not required.)

Army Form C. 2118

Place	Date	Hour	Summary of Events and Information	Remarks and references to Appendices
TOBBY Camp	28/5/	—	The A.D.M.S visited the Camp, inspected Everything — in the afternoon the Divisional Band played — The Germans shelled Very close to the Camp between 10-30 & 11. Wounding 4 patients.	Doyrah Bey. Lost.
	30/5/18	—	The D.D.M.S. 11th Corps visited the Camp. The Germans shelled the Camp at 10.30 P.M. with a H.V. gun wounding 4 patients who were already suffering from gas poisoning —	Tins + worms. Dog.
	31/5/	—	The A.D.M.S visited the Camp at 1.30 P.M. the H.T. a Brig field held their weekly Oretd. & Case defect boards. Gim. v. worms. Western	o'Grady.

140/3131

Not F.A.

Jan. 1918

COMMITTEE FOR THE
MEDICAL HISTORY OF THE WAR
Date 6 SEP 1918

WAR DIARY
or
INTELLIGENCE SUMMARY

(Erase heading not required.)

Army Form C. 2118

Place	Date	Hour	Summary of Events and Information	Remarks and references to Appendices
TUBBY CAMP W.17.d.4.7 Sheet 19. Belgian Trans.	1st JUNE 1918.	—	D.D.M.S. 2nd Corps. Visited the Skin depot. Weather fine.	OSTrady, A/C Col
	2nd	—	Church parades. Capt. Hallerton. R.A.M.C. admitted to Hosp. with Rose Measles. Many cases of metallic poisoning rec'd. up by 108th F.A. while turning rec'd. by Cairns by weed hidden - weather fine.	
	3rd	3 pm	Lt. Col. O'Grady R.A.M.C. O.C. 110th F.A. proceeded on 14 days leave to England. Major Burton R.A.M.C. assumed command of the unit.	
		4 pm	Colonel Latham (acting DDMS II Corps) + DADMS II Corps inspected Lutley Camp.	
	4th 5th 6th	2:30 pm to 5 pm	Col Roche ADMS 36th Divison inspected the Camp.	
	7th		Capt afferia R.A.M.C. attended Lutley Camp.	
	10th	8 pm	Divisional Band attended Lutley Camp.	
	11th	11 am	Capt Yuthrie M.C. R.A.M.C. discharged from Hospital + resumed duty. Col. Latta (Acting DDMS II Corps) + DADMS Corps visited Lutley Camp.	
		3-10 pm	Major General Coffin V.C. G.O.C. 36th Divon + A.D.M.S. inspected the Camp + visited patient.	
	12th		Over 100 cases of Influenza & 20 "D.Is" admitted in 24 hours.	
	13th	3 - 5 pm	Band Promenade by Divisional Band.	
	14th		Col Lattan (acting ADMS II Corps) + ADMS 36th Divisn. inspected the Camp	
		12:30 p	Col Roche ADMS 36th Divisn attended Camp + had a classification of patient for Base	
	15th	5 pm	Major General Ashby OC attended Conference of OCs F.As at ADMS office between plans and Ghatotha	
	16th	11 p	Major Smith attended 108th F.A. as member of Courts Inquiry into loss of Firearms, that at 108th F.A.	

WAR DIARY or INTELLIGENCE SUMMARY

(Erase heading not required.)

Army Form 2118

Instructions regarding War Diaries and Intelligence Summaries are contained in F.S. Regs., Part II. and the Staff Manual respectively. Title Pages will be prepared in manuscript.

Place	Date	Hour	Summary of Events and Information	Remarks and references to Appendices
Tidworth Park Camp 20.19 D.C.L.I. Sleaford	19/6/18 6 pm	—	Received Harry Hawgen from internment to patients.	See 22
	19/6/18	—	A.D.M.S. inspected the Camp.	
	21/6/18	—	Lt Col. Da Costa Grady reported his arrival from leave. U.K. + resumed command of Unit. A.B.H's R.S.S. were usually duty. Guard on men for home defect and Routine Coms. Weather fine + hot — Major Emerson left on leave 20/6 daily.	
	23/6/18	—	Regtl. gun. commt, 109th. Bgt. inspected the Camp + visited some of the men in hospital. Divine Service usual Church Parade in night.	05
	24/6/18	—	O.C. attended Conference on Coms. + on Training + system of training reinforcements was Morning on Coms. at O.R.me. 2nd Corps at 10 a.m. A.K. afternoon of the O.D.M.C. 2nd Corps detailed the rules to infantry Camp Rune. Rev. Bally reported his arrival.	22/6
	25/6/18	—	Instructed Coaches + tennis linen. Special teams for the L on Shorne, Week Rev. Wilson reported his arrival.	24/6
	26/6/18	—	Capt. Burrows, M.O., left for duty with 175 Bgd. F.A. Infantry horse emer, had this drill. Weather cool + showery	
	28/6/18	—	Lt Willen M.O.R.C. arrived on temp. duty to 77. Bgd- A.T.A. A.Gord. Had the usual weekly Coach + inspection the Camp. Inspection of the Camp with O/C maj. the 33rd Bom wit. Games + performed service — semi athletic.	26/6
	30/6/18	—	Church Service — tomorrow Monday is to be observed as a holiday.	30/6

War Diary   Appendix No 1

MEDICAL ARRANGEMENTS --- Z Hour. (major operations)

1. Officer i/c A.D.S. will immediately detail Captain MORHAM to the Bearer Post at R.20.c.1.2 and Lieut. CHAPMAN to post at R.34.c.3.1. He himself will take charge of the central post at R.28.b.6.5 (ROCHE FARM). Major CHRISTIE will proceed with 45 Bearers to A.D.S. as a temporary measure until relieved by an Officer from the 109th Field Ambulance when he will return to M.D.S.

2. Lieut. MILLER will return to M.D.S. and be attached to the Walking Wounded Post.

3. (N.C.O.& men) Each Bearer Officer will take 10 Bearers with him to Nos. 2, 3 & 4 Posts, Staff Sergt. Moffatt and 4 Bearers remaining at A.D.S.
If it is practical run the Cars up as far as the Bearer Posts, or if not to them, as far as possible.
Major CHRISTIE has detailed orders to divide up his surplus bearers amongst the posts.
Posts in need of more bearers should send to A.D.S. where a Bearer Subdivision will be held in reserve.
Capt. FULLERTON will leave 6 men of the present party at A.D.S. to act as guides.
Reserves of Dressings, Stretchers and Blankets will be held at A.D.S. and M.D.S. Only Stores and equipment absolutely necessary will be kept forward of these posts.

4. The Bearer Subdivision of the 109th Field Ambulance will proceed at once to A.D.S. under their own Officer, where they will remain until sent for by the Bearer Officers i/c Posts.

5. The Bearer Subdivision of the 108th Field Ambulance will be held in reserve at M.D.S.

6. A Haversack of Shell Dressings will be carried by each Stretcher Squad.

7. The cars of 108th and 109th Field Ambulances will be used to supplement our own. 3 Cars should be detailed for the MONT NOIR Sector and stay on that route.

NOTE. M.O's i/c Bearer Posts will make any alterations necessary and arrange themselves for local emergencies and altering conditions.

D O'Grady
Lieut-Colonel, R.A.M.C.
O.C., 110th Fd. Ambulance.

Army Form C. 2118.

WAR DIARY
or
INTELLIGENCE SUMMARY.
(Erase heading not required.)

110th Field Ambulance

Hour, Date, Place	Summary of Events and Information	Remarks and references to Appendices
Tully Camp. W.14 d.6.7. Sheet 19. 13. & France 1. June - 1916.	The Divisional Horse Show was held on the Aerodrome Proper - finished the astonic officers at 4. P.M. Conference at G.O.C.'s office re medical arrangements at 5.15PM	Appdx
2. " "	Received orders to move and Hand over to 102 F.A. 34th Division Hading over Complete by 4.30. P.M. Waiting	Log
3. " "	The Ambulance moved off for the S⁺ MARIE CAPPEL area at 7.30 A.M. Midday halt of 2 hours at DROGLANDS - Arrived at new location at 6.45PM. Major Christie allotted Billeting & men area for men.	Log.
4.45 PM. O.24 d.5.9. 3 June. 4. O.24.5.9.	Held sick smile & read out fire precautions - inspected transport & O.C. Sections inspected men's field ASonic. officers.	Log.
5. O.24 d 5.9.	Ansisted Admin. inf⁵ as medical arrangements: D⁺ Chapman C.H. - M.O.R.C. infantry was himself arrived.	Log.
6. O.24 d.5.9.	Accompanied the astonic s most dis Cal's w⁺ 5 30AM to visit the chief of médecin of the C⁺e tranal Corps whom we were to take over from. Waited a finish - sent party of M.C.O's to Rossignol to settle arrangements for taking over tomorrow. Sent guides for the Infantry own.	Log.

WAR DIARY
or
INTELLIGENCE SUMMARY
(Erase heading not required.)

Army Form C. 2118

Place	Date	Hour	Summary of Events and Information	Remarks and references to Appendices
O.24.d.5.9	7	8 A.M.	Detailed parties for different A.D.S's — situated at MONT NOIR M.20.c.1.2. ROCH FARM R.26.c.7.T. — Farm at R.34.c.3.1. and at ROSSIGNOL R.22.c.7.T. The Ration parts in the main leave never both Car Stand of well as the ADS's.	
D.24.d.5.9	7	3.30 P.M.	Ambulance moved off for new site. HdQ's take at Q.22-c.3.1 while in late made ready to light as an main Dressing Station. The parties for Convoys to Q.22.c.3.1 in Horsed Ambulances & motors were the ADS's.	
Q.22.c.3.1	7	5.15 P.M.	Arrived at new site. The Horsed Drawn coy are still in possession of the buildings & huts.	
" "	7	9. P.M.	Parties moved off for ADS's. Capt-Fullerton M.C. to ROCH FARM. Capt MILLER, MORE. to MONT NOIR and Capt MOREHAM RAMC to R.34.c.3.1. Each with 16 N.C.O's & men and 2 wheeled Stretchers, weather fine. Staff Sergt MOFFAT, in charge of Rossignol post.	
" "	8	11 AM.	ADS's visited. Our camp and ADS's visited me - most of the wood are in derelict ruins of the Convoy so all until the huts drawn at night — The morale of the posts of Rd section table 4 in horses.	
" "	9	9 AM.	Conveyed duties for misters. Sent parties to salve wood & then to make hut. misters Rossignol, post at 9.30 P.M. builders	
" "	10	-	Using nights the Count & our fuels, building & early	

WAR DIARY
or
INTELLIGENCE SUMMARY
(Erase heading not required.)

Army Form C. 2118

Place	Date	Hour	Summary of Events and Information	Remarks and references to Appendices
Q.2.C.9.1.	11th	--	Under Instructions from the A.D.M.S., the three officers at the A.D.S. were recalled to the "Rossignol." Three being already the M.O's of the Supporting Batt. at the A.D.S. The Field Ambulance Officers & men have taken the Post at – in Rossignol under Capt. Fullerton, M.C. from to 5th	
" " "	12.	"	The Unit has 15 minutes air gas drill every morning at 7 A.M. The A.D.M.S. visited the advanced posts during the night	to 5th
" " "	13th	"	Visited the advanced posts with Capt. Fullerton. Had fine drills of practice gas alarm. Arranged for scheme of evacuation in the event of Adrian operations – copies of which were attached.	p.g.
" " "	14th	--	A.D.M.S. visited the A.D.S. and advanced posts during the night at 6.30. P.M. & Horti's Shell burst near the Camp – many pieces flying the truck & hut – no casualties.	to 5th p.g.
" " "	15.	"	The Mont-row Sector I recognised the roads – the trucks & roads in this Sector are particularly bad in Infantile, for motor Camp with wheeled stretchers in 5 kilometres – over bad ground. p.g.	
" " "	16.	"	Party at Ad. Q's all employed building Huts & clearing out generally spent a Gas Centre with trucks & one Hut to accomodate 30 patients. p.g.	

WAR DIARY
or
INTELLIGENCE SUMMARY
(Erase heading not required.)

Army Form C. 2118

Place	Date	Hour	Summary of Events and Information	Remarks and references to Appendices
Q22,c,5,1	17th	—	The ADMS visited the Camp and Rode the advanced posts, & R.APs. the Reserves at the Relay Posts & R.a.P's and being relieved any this day, then at Rossignol every 2 waters.	App.
		4.P.M	The D.D.M.S X Corps visited the Camp.	Weather Cloudy
	18th	—	Visited the advanced Posts of the XI-Section — arranged for the setting up of Dressing Signs to A.D.S, Hell & the Drill Cop.t MOREHAM was relieved by Jr. Clapham	App.
	19th	......	Visited the A.D.M.S. the Medical arrangements, & Corps Came carried from 108th T.A.	App.
	20th	....	D.M.S. 2nd Army visited the Camp with the D.M.S x Corps + A.D.M.S. 36th Division — He was satisfied. Visited the advanced Posts — weather wild.	App.
	21st		Usual Church Service	App.
	22nd	—	ADMS visited the Camp. I visited the Rossignol post will were slightly mild.	App.
	23rd		4 of my learners at Mont Noir were sent down gassed. Apparently "Mustard" gas. The Germans were particularly active during the night 23rd – 24th. —	App.

WAR DIARY or INTELLIGENCE SUMMARY

Army Form C. 2118

(Erase heading not required.)

Instructions regarding War Diaries and Intelligence Summaries are contained in F.S. Regs., Part II. and the Staff Manual respectively. Title Pages will be prepared in manuscript.

Place	Date	Hour	Summary of Events and Information	Remarks and references to Appendices
Q.22.C.30	24th	—	The ADMS visited the advanced posts. Grinsted Rossignol Hall. Gun alarm practice at N4-Q4. —	
	25th 26—	—	Visited the 103rd F.A. who were working at the B.R.S. nightly. work parties — G.S. waggons are carrying Hilis from the forward area for B.R.S. & assembled the reads near Beerhalpe, in the Ott sanitation work from Mont Moir. weather wet. Post.	
	27—	—	Advd visited the Camp. Work of the Work at main B.S. have also formed the W-W-C-R and arrangements were made by afping for a light rly midway between its own for W.W. in at- Q 26. 13. 9.8 — the entraining heglined— were not— park for W.W. in at- Q 26. 13. 9.8 —	Post.
	28—	—	Visited the advanced posts at work party at BERTHEN. Arrange number of wounded coming through. 8. nightly. Spire was taken ever the Area — Unial Church Services W—	post.
	29—	—	Attended Conference at ADMS Offices. Discussed medical arrangements in the event of Hostile Attack etc — ADMS visited the Advanced posts — weather fine	Post.

1875 Wt. W593/826 1,000,000 4/15 J.B.C. & A. A.D.S.S./Forms/C. 2118.

WAR DIARY
or
INTELLIGENCE SUMMARY

(Erase heading not required.)

Army Form C. 2118

Place	Date	Hour	Summary of Events and Information	Remarks and references to Appendices
Q 22,2,3,1	7th 30		Inspected the Advanced Galli with Capt. Fullerton - Army Troy Satisfactory - trafrulis hoved lively at Camps generally very heft.	Ref.
" " "	31st	...	Inspected Camps. Horse lines + held a gun alarm practice at 11 A.M. - Wouther very Hot.	Bitfandy At Col.

War Diary.   MEDICAL ARRANGEMENTS.   Appendix No 1.
                             110th Field Ambulance.

Reference maps   The evacuation from the R.A.P. is being carried out
27 S.E. &   in the forward sector by Wheeled Stretchers on which the
28.S.W.   patients are brought back to the Bearer Relay Posts.
                     From these posts Motor Ambulance Cars clear cases every
                     night to the A.D.S. In the event of a case requiring
                     immediate Hospital treatment, a message should be sent
                     to the A.D.S. for a Motor Ambulance. This is the only
                     time that a Motor Ambulance is allowed to work in the
                     forward area except at night (9.30 p.m. to 5 a.m.).

Map References.

Main Dressing Station   )   Q.22.c.3.1
Hd.Qrs.Field Ambulance   )
A.D.S. & Car Stand   R.20.7.7
Bearer Relay Posts.
MONT NOIR   M.20.c.1.2
ROCHE FARM   R.28.b.6.5
                                                 R.29.d.2.2
Bearer Posts at
   R.A.P's   M.26.b.1.2
     "   (Chateau Blanch)   M.32.a.2.3
     "   R.34.c.3.1
     "   X.5.a.3.2
Advanced Car Stand.   R.34.c.3.1

     Casualties will be cleared from R.A.P. under the
control of the Officer i/c Bearer Division, who has for
this purpose 9 Wheeled Stretchers and 4 Large Motor
Ambulance Cars.
     The following routes will be used by Bearers and Cars
from R.A.P's to A.D.S.
RIGHT SECTOR.
     (a) Road from KOPJE FARM to SCHAAXKEN and across to IBEX
         Cottage straight to A.D.S. ROSSIGNOL.
     (b) Road from Chateau Blanch (M.22.a.2.8) to LA MANCHE
         through MANCHE Copse to Main road to BERTHEN turning
         left at R.22.c.5.8 and to ROSSIGNOL.
     (c) Alternative path from MANCH Copse by track running
         in a curve through R.29 A & C Squares along line of
         trees joining main BERTHEN Road at R.28 central.

LEFT SECTOR.
     (a) Road from R.A.P. M.26.b.1.2 to MONT NOIR Relay Post
         continuing down track to PUDEFORT past STAIRS HOUSE
         to Main Road passing Mt.KOKEREELE turning Right at
         GATE CORNER, first turn to Left from Main Road on
         road running through R.15 A & B, thence past Divisional
         Headquarters through CANTA CORNER to Main Dressing
         Station at Q.22.c.3.1.
         NOTE. This route is not yet ready for traffic, so
         the evacuation will be through BERTHEN.

     From A.D.S. all cases will be evacuated by night to M.D.SS
except urgent cases which will be moved at once.
     Cases from MONT NOIR Post will be evacuated direct to
M.D.S. not touching the A.D.S. at all.

WALKING WOUNDED.
The forward area will be flagged at Cross Roads with
directing boards pointing towards and marked A.D.S. with
the Divisional Sign and a Red Cross.

A.T. SERUM.
A.T. Serum will be given at the A.D.S. and A.F.W. 3118 made out, until ZERO hour, when this will be done at the M.D.S. ZERO hour will be when any major operations commence.

SICK COLLECTION.
Sick in the back areas will be collected by Horsed Ambulances from M.D.S. Those in the Forward Area must be evacuated in the same way as wounded.

SELF INFLICTED WOUNDS.
All Self Inflicted and Accidentally Wounded must have the fact recorded on their A.F.A.3210 and Field Medical Card.

CARE OF OFFICERS KITS.
Instructions laid down in D.G.M.S. G.H.Q. No.G.D./2 dated 10th May 1915 will be thoroughly carried out.
Only kits brought in at the same time as the Officers will be received; any arriving later will be returned to the Officers Unit.

CASES OF DEATHS AT A.D.S.
These will be notified by the quickest means to the M.D.S. who will despatch the necessary notifications.

PERSONNEL RELIEFS.
A.D.S. reliefs will be arranged every 2 weeks as far as possible, one half at a time to allow the incoming bearers to pick up the work.
Bearer Posts. Every Week.
Regimental Bearer Posts. Every 4 days.

D. de C. O'Grady
Lieut-Colonel, RR.A.M.C.
O.C. 110th Field Ambulance.

140/3200.

COMMITTEE FOR
MEDICAL HISTORY
Date 5 OCT 1916

110" 4. a.

Aug. 1918.

WAR DIARY or INTELLIGENCE SUMMARY

Army Form C. 2118

110 2nd Army No. 35

Place	Date August	Hour	Summary of Events and Information	Remarks and references to Appendices
Q.22.c.1.3.	1/8	"	The A.D.M.S. visited the Camp with reference to Medical Arrangements for the coming operations & visited the A.D.S. which has been shelled by the Enemy — Capt. Fullerton went to Bazuel close by — there were several Casualties from transport on the road — the horses at Rossignol badly damaged.	Ref nearby
" " "	3/8	"	Capt. Morison relieved Capt. Fullerton at A.D.S. Capt. Fullerton M.O. was detailed to represent the Division at the 14th Anniversary of the service practice parade held today at E.K.R.G.	ref.
" " "	4/8	"	Usual Church Services — Capt. Fullerton & other ranks Bn from the 3 field Ambulances attended the Anniversary Service at Div H.Q's. I visited the A.D.S. during the night.	Bref.
" " "	5/8	"	I visited the A.D.S. Rossignol at 4 P.M. — then a short visit to forward positions — during the night — Weather fine.	ref.
" " "	7/8	"	I visited the forward area the night & was out ag/65a leaves to most novi service on avenue, after difficulty of surmounting Around visited the M.D.S. & forward area — home.	ref.
" " "	8/8		Visited the A.D.S. and the A.D.S. seen officer re medical Arrangements — the Enemy's Artillery is getting very active many shells dropping in the neighbourhood of the M.D.S. farm.	ref

WAR DIARY or INTELLIGENCE SUMMARY

Army Form C. 2118

Place	Date	Hour	Summary of Events and Information	Remarks and references to Appendices
Q.22.C.1.3.	10/5/18	—	Held fire drill & inspected Camp - Horse lines - Mont-noir sentries were shelled during the night. Sergt. Gailey & Private Robinson. H. were badly gassed while lunging in & Robinson died at M.D.S. Walter gunner wounded [illegible]	Sgt.
	11/5/18	—	Sgt. Gailey died from effects of gas poisoning in 62. C.C.S. Funeral the funeral party to numerate at the casualties - No 2 post Rock gunner was not will left in command for entry Church Service. Capt. W.H. Sutcliffe reported for duty. Major Russell O/C 109# T.A. reported his arrival for duty at A.D.S. - relieving Capt. Fullerton.	Sgt.
	13/5/18	"	A Divisional Ambulance judging Shows & Chose 2 Ambulance Waggon - Water Carts is represent the Divisional in the Competition - 109th-T.A. 110-T.A. 101 T.A.	Sgt.
	14/5/18	"	During the night 13/14. the enemy put over a lot of gas shells principally yellow cross. Several working party were caught & were admitted including 4 officers. They waited the 62. C.C.S. by midnight 56 of 143 cases were sent to C.C.S. including the trench cases - twins expected. Lt. Chapman M.O.R.C. proceeded to 1st Roy field Ambulance for temp duty.	Sgt.
	15/5/18		Capt. Sutcliffe proceeded to 9. Roy field Ambulance for temp duty - Trench & G.S. activities - 108th & the 109th waiting work	Sgt.

WAR DIARY or INTELLIGENCE SUMMARY

Army Form C. 2118

Place	Date	Hour	Summary of Events and Information	Remarks and references to Appendices
Q.22, C.1.3	16/8/18	—	Capt Coghlan reported his arrival for temp duty from 109th F.A. as the A.D.S. — heavy shelling on front & back areas — several mules of Carnoy killed — W.O. moved but from 109 — 3 field ambulances provided for temporary duty to 1 Royal Irish Rifles. O.B.M.S. went to forward posts. Lieut W.J Hanberly M.O.R.C. reported his arrival for duty.	807
" "	18/8/18		Tonight the A.D.S. and bearer posts were attempting everything possible. Stretchers — the movements to mobile farm proposed it made it safer for 26th Stretcher Cases & also that it may be used as an When Rossignol would be to from death. Weatherhill Ontis, when noise is — Army the Camps.	
" "	21/8/18	"	Aid-Post. W.O. rejoined from Celis — The 1st Royal Irish Rifles and proceeded to 15-R.Y-R. for temp duty — the Battalion on the night sector objective Maurepas Ferran + trenches M + E of it — attached with, attack completely successful & many 1 hour - at-12.30 A.M. 21st - 22nd advanced posts with the bearer officer. 3 Casualties — the O.B.M.S. was at the advance posts. The medical arrangements proved simple.	
	23/8/18	"	Invited the A.D.S. + advanced posts. O.B.M.S. went more advance medical arrangements — Advanced posts in left section by Messrs Sinclair & Churchill. June	807

WAR DIARY or INTELLIGENCE SUMMARY

Army Form C. 2118

Place	Date	Hour	Summary of Events and Information	Remarks and references to Appendices
Q.21.c.1.5	24/8/18	1.A.M.	Zero hour for an attack on a 1000 yds front. Opposite our right/really R.A.P.'s were moved up to our new line. Thunder during the night 4 officer casualties & 69 other ranks — 10 gunners were evacuated through M.D.S. All arrangements were good & no hitch occurred. Marked the difficulty of getting M.O. e came. The A. Bde. were all advanced posts with Major Russell during the attack. The 26th Division visited by A.D.S. & M.O.'s. A.Divns.	Sig.
	26/8/18		A.Bde. & O.C. 105 F.A. 26th Division visited by A.D.S. & M.O.g. A.Divns. weather fine & cold.	Sig.
	27/9/18		Received orders to take over X Corps Rest Station at "PELDEAHOECK". Sheet 27. Belgian & French, arranged with D.O. 105 F.A. G.15.a.37. for the taking over of the forward posts on 28 & 29. Arrangements made with O.C. 105 F.A. the advanced posts.	Sig.
	28/8/18		O.C. 105 — visited on sig. & ADS's, with me — all arrangements completed — weather showery & cold.	Sig.
	29/8/18		Sent forward some waggons & kit. All bearers & officers returned to M.D.S. Major Russell & Capt Conyers report their detachments for duty F.A. 109 F.A.	Watts Slowery. Sig.
G.15.A.5.9 Sheet 27 Pat 7	30/8/18	8 A.M. 6 P.M.	The field ambulance moved off from the X Corps Rest Station at G.15.2.5.9 arrived at 6 P.M. Men & horses marshalled. Belgian & French. Well. Attended Conference at A.D.M.S. office at 11 P.M. fine	Sig.

WAR DIARY
or
INTELLIGENCE SUMMARY

(Erase heading not required.)

Army Form C. 2118

Place	Date	Hour	Summary of Events and Information	Remarks and references to Appendices
G.16.a.5.9.	31/12	10 A.M	Further instructions received from A Dins. The Ambulance moved off for "Oehtegesele". The Divisional Rest Station - H.29.d.4.8. Sheet 27, 1/40.	
H.29.d.4.8.	31/12	1.P.M	Arrived, taking over convoyed by 3 P.M. when 108th Field Ambulance moved off. Visited the admg. officer in the afternoon. Corps Horse Show was held at Terdeghem. & this Ambulance sent open to all Corps divisions to attend. Howd. Ambulance & Walter Carl. won the Germans Ambulance relaying along the whole divisional front. Refusal.	

WAR DIARY
or
INTELLIGENCE SUMMARY

Army Form C. 2118

110 Fd Amb

Vol 37

Place	Date	Hour	Summary of Events and Information	Remarks and references to Appendices
GOMMECOURT H.29.D.4.8.	1/7/18	-	Sunday - Usual Church service. C. of E, Cof S, Cof I, Chaplain presided at 3.20 full parade. Capt Fullerton reported his arrival from leave.	S.31
	3/7/18	-	Time drills and inspection of A Sections harness and equipment. A Sect is in clothing & cleaning mode, equipment visited a Div'l officers which have now moved to St Jeans Capelle, near Bailleul. The Germans are retiring rapidly by Capt Moreham & C. & A.D.S Tunnell returned from leave. Weather fine.	S.32
	4/7/18	-	I visited the main dressing station which is at Rod farm R.22.B.5.6. There are not many casualties there there are nearly all walking gun wounds. Capt Moreham went for temporary duty to M.DS. Huntscott retuning. Weather fine -	OUT
	6/7/18	-	I am gradually moving the equipment of the B.I.R.S. down to the site of the old M.DS. now "Elthé" at Q.22.C.1.3. whilst in lieu the new - B.I.R.S. I visited the A.D.M.S office and a D.C. offering medical arrangements discussed finer settling jobs.	
	7/18	-	Lieut Chapman M.O.R.C. left for temporary duty with 109.F.A. during the night of 6th-7th Staff Serjt moffatt returned to duty as Acting Sgt. A.B.of.	
	8/7/18	-	Handed over charge of Ambulance to Capt Fullerton - M.C. & proceeded on Leave in France	S.33

Army Form C. 2118

WAR DIARY
or
INTELLIGENCE SUMMARY
(Erase heading not required.)

Instructions regarding War Diaries and Intelligence Summaries are contained in F.S. Regs., Part II. and the Staff Manual respectively. Title Pages will be prepared in manuscript.

Place	Date	Hour	Summary of Events and Information	Remarks and references to Appendices
GHYVELDE H.29.d.2.4.5	9/2/18	"	Col. Zeppelin L. Sector. 1 Section detached off duty in hospital to clean & check vol. equipment	appx
	10/2/18	"	Inspection of L section in full marching order	appx
	12/2/18	"	Hospital equipment being moved to 108 F. Amb. as it can be dispensed with.	appx
	15/2/18	"	Church services as usual	appx
	16/2/18	"	Major Chadels returned from leave	appx
	17/2/18	"	Capt Appleton took over charge of 2nd of R' Corps Scheme. meeting	appx
	18/2/18	"	Capt Appleton took over charge of Chinese Labour Camp WESTOUS CAPPEL	appx
	20/2/18	"	A.D.M.S. 3U Div inspected hospital arrangements various suggestions	appx
	"	"	O.C. 110 F. Field Amb returned from Leave (French)	
	22/2/18	"	Appleton reported to 108 F. Amb for duty	appx
	24/2/18	"	Handed over Regt Centre at Ochtezeele to 109 Field Amb & move to St Jan de Bezgen Major Chester reported at 89. F.C.	appx

WAR DIARY
or
INTELLIGENCE SUMMARY
(Erase heading not required.)

Army Form C. 2118

Instructions regarding War Diaries and Intelligence Summaries are contained in F.S. Regs., Part II. and the Staff Manual respectively. Title Pages will be prepared in manuscript.

Place	Date	Hour	Summary of Events and Information	Remarks and references to Appendices
ST JAN DE BIEZEN	27/8/18		Moved to OMALIA FARM. Capt Connor reported for temporary duty	ack
	28/8/18		One Officer & 50 O.R. from 16/M.I.R. reported for duty. stretcher bearers. 2 enemy moved to School. 4 P&c.S. leaving transport behind under Lt. I. M. Pernell	ack
YPRES	29/8/18		This morning Capt Tollerton in charge of transport & sick moved up the line to establish feeds taken in the O.C. impulse than feeds	

A.S. Christopher
M.J.E. Lyon
for O.C. in the field.

COMMITTEE FOR THE
MEDICAL HISTORY OF THE WAR
4 DEC. 1918
Date

WAR DIARY
or
INTELLIGENCE SUMMARY
(Erase heading not required.)

Army Form C. 2118

Instructions regarding War Diaries and Intelligence Summaries are contained in F.S. Regs., Part II. and the Staff Manual respectively. Title Pages will be prepared in manuscript.

Vol 39.

Place	Date	Hour	Summary of Events and Information	Remarks and references to Appendices
School House YPRES	1/10/16	—	Visited posts. Transport arrived from Gwalia Farm & were parked behind the School House. Weather wet	100 party
"	3/10/16	—	Arranged to collect the sick of the 36 D.W. from the II Corps. Walking Wounded Station and transfer to 108 Fd Amb.	9657
"	5/10/16	—	Capt E.F.R. CONDER R.A.M.C. proceed to 109 Fd Ambr for duty	9087
"	6/10/16	—	Visited A.D.M.S.	1107
"	7/10/16	—	Inspected A.D. Station and Bearer Posts. Field Ambulance with Transport moved to Infantry Barracks YPRES. Town heavily shelled. Major A.M.S. CHRISTIE and party rejoined from 89 Fd Amb. Weather fair.	
Infantry Bks. YPRES	8/10/16	—	Capt C.F.R. CONDER joined for temporary duty. Lieut. C.A. WHITFIELD R.A.M.C. joined for duty from Base and taken on strength of unit. Capt A. FULLERTON M.C. came down to Hd qrs for a rest. together with the majority of bearers from behind line	To 857
"	9/10/16	—	A.D.M.S. invited camp. Capt CONDER proceeded to A.D.S.	To 857
"	10/10/16	—	Major A.W.S. CHRISTIE took over A.D.S. and Capt CONDER took charge of the Loon Stand.	857
"	11/10/16	—	20 Other Ranks 16 R.S. Rifles (P.) reported for duty	10857

WAR DIARY or INTELLIGENCE SUMMARY

Army Form C. 2118

Place	Date	Hour	Summary of Events and Information	Remarks and references to Appendices
Infantry Barracks Y PRES	12/10/18	—	Transport under Lieut. C.A. WHITFIELD moved to Gwalia Farm. Remainder of unit proceeded to A.D.S. BECELAERE.	
BECELAERE	14/10/18	—	Opened M.D.S. at Becelaere. In the afternoon moved M.D.S. up to DADIZEELE. Weather fine. Wounded passed through Officers 45. O.R. 930. (approx)	
DADIZEELE	15/10/18		do 11 " 20 " 360	
"	16/10/18		do —	
"	17/10/18		do 20 " 160	
	18/10/18		Handed over M.D.S. to 138 Field Ambce and moved to LEDEGHEM. Wounded passed through Officers Nil O.R. 25	
LEDEGHEM	19/10/18	—	Field Ambulance less transport moved from LEDEGHEM to LENDELEDE. Passed through Officers 2. O.R. 33. Wounded.	
			Capt A FULLERTON and 4 A6 O.R. proceeded to various Batt'ns 9/10/Bde. Wounded Admitted. Officers 9 O.R. 143.	
LENDELEDE	20/10/18		Lieut. C.A. WHITFIELD proceeded for temporary duty with 1st R Ir Fus. 18 Other Ranks from 109 Field Amb'ce proceeding to Advanced Dressing	
"	21/10/18		Centre and were detained for the night. Wounded admitted. Officers 8. O.R. 106.	
	22/10/18	—	Transport joined unit from LEDEGHEM. Wounded admitted Officers 10. O.R. 135.	

WAR DIARY
or
INTELLIGENCE SUMMARY
(Erase heading not required.)

Army Form C. 2118

Place	Date	Hour	Summary of Events and Information	Remarks and references to Appendices
LENDELEDE	23/10/18		30 Other Ranks. 16 R.I. Rifles (P) reported for duty. Wounded admitted Officer 1 OR 40	Apy
"	24/10/18		" " 2 " 18	Apy
"	25/10/18		Advanced Party proceeded to DEERLYCK. 1 WCO and 20 men from 16 R.I. Rifles (P) reported for duty. Bearer parties proceeded to various units of the Brigade. Wounded admitted Officers 6. O.R. 136.	Apy
DEERLYCK	26/10/18	10 am	Night Staff proceeded to DEERLYCK to open M.D.S. Day Staff followed in Afternoon. Bearer parties returned from the Brigade in the evening. Wounded admitted Officers 3. O.R. 60. Village shelled during the night.	Apy
"	27/10/18		16 R.I. Rifles (P) partly rejoined their unit. Wounded admitted Officers nil O.R. 14	Apy
AELBEKE	28/10/18		Unit moved to AELBEKE took over from 107 Fd Ambre 34 Div. Transport rejoined the unit. Collected Sick from units of the Brigade. Local units and bearer parties then to 108 Fd Amb. Div. Command ADMS visited the unit.	Apy
"	29/10/18			Apy

J.S. Noble Capt. 36 D.

1046/011

Siberia.

110 F + a

COMMITTEE FOR THE
MEDICAL HISTORY OF THE WAR.
Date: 16 JAN 1919

WAR DIARY
or
INTELLIGENCE SUMMARY.
(Erase heading not required.)

Army Form C. 2118.

110 2n Amb

Place	Date	Hour	Summary of Events and Information	Remarks and references to Appendices
AELBEKE	2/4/18	—	Received Warning Order that Brigade would move from present area	
"	3/4/18	3pm	2d Amb to move under orders of 104 Brigade. Proceeded to MOUSCRON. Capt Fullerton had arranged accommodation in the Convent Notre Dame.	
MOUSCRON	4/4/18		Arranged to take over two floors of one block of buildings for use as Hospital.	
"	5/4/18		Counties of Ostend worked convent with a view to opening Civilian Hospital	
"	6/4/18		Opened hospital for skin cases. Took over all cases from D.S. Rest Station (104 FA)	
"	8/4/18		ADMS visited the unit	
"	9/4/18		Attended ADMS office and all 2d Commanders and arranged details of combined church parade	
"	10/4/18	2:30pm	Combined Church Parade for 3 FAs in Theatre of Convent. ADMS attended and afterwards inspected parade and thanked officers + OR for their good work during recent operations	

WAR DIARY
or
INTELLIGENCE SUMMARY.
(Erase heading not required.)

Army Form C. 2118.

Place	Date	Hour	Summary of Events and Information	Remarks and references to Appendices
Mouscron	17/8/18	07.00	Handed over charge to Major A.W.S. Christie & proceeded on leave	
	17/8/18	10.30	Attended church parade with 108 T.M. O.D.M.S. attended	
	18/18		A.D.M.S visited 9 infantry hospital	
	20/8	13.00	D.M.S Second army conference of D.D.M.S. & Corps ₹ D.M.S. 2nd Air inspected the Unit D.M.S. discussed various form work done whilst with 2nd Army	
	24/8	09.30	Attd first church parade with 108 & 109 T.A.	
			A.D.M.S attended	
	28/8	15.30	D.M.S infantry hospital	
			All Christian Army troops 110 TA Army 110 TA	
	2/9/18	-	O.C. Lt Col Dole C.O'Grady - returned from leave. Health well Reports	
	29/9	-	Visited the Dental officer.	
	30/9	-	The D.M.S XV Corps with A Brig 3.6 - known has visited the hospital - All then over to y to C.S.O. visited Lt Col	

Sd/Signed Lt Col
O.C. 110 T.A.

No. 110. F.A.

Dec. 1918

WAR DIARY or INTELLIGENCE SUMMARY

Army Form C. 2118.

110th Inf. Amm[unition] 1st Aug [?] Vol 39

Place	Date	Hour	Summary of Events and Information	Remarks and references to Appendices
Mouveau	1/9/18		A Church Service attended Church Service at 11.20 A.M. other services as usual - afternoon interested the Enemy bale + divisional Mass. A Sacred Concert was held at St Joseph Hall at 5.20.	App[x]
	2/9/18		All units resumed to parade for instruction by the Brigade Commander	App[x]
	3/9/18		3rd Inst. L.D. line drill & Musketry. 4th (etc) the Hospice. All this parade — Inspectional ? — Inspected the same lines and Ammo parade football last night — weather wet	App[x]
	4/9/18	11"	As usual. The Hospice was a long line — Finer winds held at 1.30 under Stan S.O. — Better wet	App[x]
	6/9/18		A practice parade will be held Various brass in HALSUN turnout — Include a parade at 6 A.M.	App[x]
	7/9/18	12"	Wrist past - Divisional parade at 7.5 AM - Inspection held by Divisional Commander — divisional Band in attendance at 4.30 PM —	App[x]
	9/9/18		A.M.E. visited the Hospital & Love River — Station man — out a parade to Concealing Memorial dinner — Church Services as usual, Army attended C. of E. Service	App[x]

WAR DIARY
or
INTELLIGENCE SUMMARY.
(Erase heading not required.)

Army Form C. 2118.

Instructions regarding War Diaries and Intelligence Summaries are contained in F. S. Regs., Part II. and the Staff Manual respectively. Title pages will be prepared in manuscript.

Place	Date	Hour	Summary of Events and Information	Remarks and references to Appendices
Marylebone	9/12/18		The undermentioned Commdg. Were informed by the General Institution	
			1st Col. D.&Co. G. READY — Frank Crony de Guerner a Jordan C.B.Ps. (gild/a)	
			Major A.W.S Clarke — " " " " R(W)(A) (Bunge)	
			Lt Col W- Parnell — " " " " " " "	
	10/12/18		Infantry Sch. Strafford and Stalker	207
			O.R.Ms. Knopfler & Ruthafrd & Dunning	
	11/12/18		Sectional equipment will be Elaborated by the 19-hut install. — sides	207
			Ceremonial parade by Corps Commander at Hallow on the 12.12.18	
			Orders from Bude found to be Good	
	12/12/18		Went off as far as the Staking but when the above parade or	207
			cancelled — raining and wet. A&nd visited the unit	
	13/12/18		The Divisional Commander presented Brevet & Imeural Medals	207
			to the R&ME Unit — A&ms G&ms C&ms 1081, 1087 F.A.	
			in Marruitt	
			A&ms attended Divine Service at 11.30. afternoon	Sig 8/1
	15/12/18		Holbrook & Dunning off Services as usual	
			went on leave	207

WAR DIARY or INTELLIGENCE SUMMARY

Army Form C. 2118.

(Erase heading not required.)

Place	Date	Hour	Summary of Events and Information	Remarks and references to Appendices
Moislains Area	16/12/18		The Corps Commander inspected the Divisions at Halloin at 11.30	857
"	17/12/18		Bent word that he was placed under Orders at 24 hrs. notice –	857
	18/12/18		Divs visited the Hospital & Stables – with Brody –	857
	19/12/18		Manifolds the troops, soldiers + Stables – Held a pow wow at 2 p.m.—	857
			again settled in the afternoon —	
	21/12/18		C.O. inspected the Divn. at 14.50 – Principal order to the Corps	857
			Commander arranging of festivities need out. Also a Nominal Warning	
	22/12/18		Usual Church Services – the Officers attended the C. of E. Service	857
			afterwards impromptu Dinner	857
	23/12/18		Inspected the Horses. Genl Coffin V.C. & A.D.C.? will attend	
			led the Xmas Parade & wished us all a happy Christmas	857
	24/12/18		Spent in Preparation for Christmas day	857
	25/12/18		Christmas day – Usual Church Service with Special Hymns	
			The R.M.O. Inspected Dinners + Wounds + wished them to all	
	26/12/18		have a day off Christmas	857
			Return to Work	

WAR DIARY
INTELLIGENCE SUMMARY

Army Form C. 2118.

Place	Date	Hour	Summary of Events and Information	Remarks and references to Appendices
Mooltan	27/12		Major-A Fullerton M.C. R.I.F. [?] on leave — O'Grady in charge — Duggan[?] — this day was full — nine O.R.s Patients — day of the death inquiry of W.B. Sproul	
	28/12		& Hollis play'd during the afternoon	
	29/12		Buffoli — Hospital — attack by Corp. Michael Mullen[?] Medical Officer Received O.R. ns attended during Service	
	30/12		& visited Barracks etc —	
	31/12		O.R.s inspected the Hospital & divisions Went daily for exercise & Patrols Ration made with Guns & attended on parade —	

T. O'Grady Lt.Col.
O.C. 110 F.A.

10/76/91

No. 110 F.A.

Jan. 1919

COMMITTEE FOR THE
MEDICAL HISTORY OF THE WAR
CANK 919

Army Form C. 2118.

WAR DIARY
or
INTELLIGENCE SUMMARY.
(Erase heading not required.)

36 DIV
Box 2298

Instructions regarding War Diaries and Intelligence Summaries are contained in F. S. Regs., Part II. and the Staff Manual respectively. Title pages will be prepared in manuscript.

Place	Date	Hour	Summary of Events and Information	Remarks and references to Appendices
MOUSCRON	1919			
	1/1/18		Took over temporary command of Field Ambulance from the Col O'Gorman who proceeded on leave	
	6/1/9		A.D.M.S. inspected hospital	app 1
	10/1/9		D.M.S. inspected hospital	app 2
	11/1/9		Lt. Parnell proceeded on leave	app 3
	11/1/9		Attended meeting of XV Corps Medical Society at Menin – met with our Col	apps 4
	12/1/9		R.C.M.S. inspected hospital	app 5
	13/1/9		Major Talbot representative of ???? from leave	app 6
	15/1/9		A.D.M.S. inspected hospital	
	17/1/9		Lt. Col. O'Gorman returned from leave	
			A.W. Christie Major	
	17/1/9		Returned from leave & took over command from Major Christie with fire & freezing	
	19/1/9		A.D.M.S. visited the hospital & inspected the Wards	Wholly app 7

WAR DIARY
or
INTELLIGENCE SUMMARY.

(Erase heading not required.)

Army Form C. 2118.

110 2nd Aust

19

Place	Date	Hour	Summary of Events and Information	Remarks and references to Appendices
MONCHERON	19/9		Colonel Roch DSO on left for leave in England 1 month - yr Col. D.A.C. O'GRADY in acting command.	
	21/9		Half the brick still about to be trans[ferred] to your own[?] Hospital.	
	23/9		Inspection the Unit at 2 P.M. Supply of boots & leather feel[t] rifle & the new boots are not a bad issue. Arms the Horsfield cases inspected by Major General Captain - V.C. D.S.O.	
	25/9			
	27/9		Attend at A.D.M.S. Office daily at 11-30 - Inspected Horse Lines & mess Orgs Satisfactory - snow	
	29/9		Hun Pride - 11-30 - Int Panville Infantry	
	31/9		Renewed Ganseavity from leave. Showing H.R.H. Captain the Prince of Wales invited the Unit - with Major-Captain V.C. ? company	

[signature] O.C. 110 F.A.

No. 110 Field Ambulance.

WAR DIARY
or
INTELLIGENCE SUMMARY.
(Erase heading not required.)

Army Form C. [2118]

110 FA

Vol 4

Place	Date	Hour	Summary of Events and Information	Remarks and reference to Appendices
Aberdeen	2/4/19		Held a batt inspection & visited ADms office	Appdx 1
	3		Time spent in moving & visiting [commands] Plan to return to ADms office - Returned in Voluntering for Army of Occupation - Army of [Occupation]	
	5/4/19		Checked equipment by soldiers - Look thro the BC [returned] and inspected BBts - which ant now died & more come up written in the [Returns] on returns	Appx
	7/4/19		Visited ADms office	Appx
	8/4/19		Had a [parade] 9 - 11 a.m. Inspected personnel - re clothing	Appx
	9/4/19		Attended ADms office of which we had [returned] men on [return] and [visiting] Supplement details -	Appx
	11/4/19		Fine Above and Visited ([Practice])	Appx
	12/4/19		Visited ADms office in morning took Officers to horse [lines]	Appx
	14/4/19		Visited ADms office - [report] to Horse lines	Appx
	15/4/19		Inspected hospital in morning & visited ADms office in afternoon -	Appx

WAR DIARY
or
INTELLIGENCE SUMMARY.
(Erase heading not required.)

Army Form C. 2118

Place	Date	Hour	Summary of Events and Information	Remarks and references to Appendices
Maresbergen	18/9		Nine (9) Officers returning from an [unclear] lecture to	
"	19/9		enjoining - Fire drill & series of signals. Clerks [unclear]	95f
"	21/9		United Officers Officers Quiet Stores Horse Lines	
"			United Officers Officers held a farewell luncheon in	98f
"	23/9		the evening to Officers to all.	
"	25/9		United Officers Officers supplied a Guards with	99f
"	28/9²		Iam on leave in France. Hand over to Major Christie	100f
			A.D.M.S. inspection completed	Auts

Christie
Maj Christie
Arty 110 Falconer

140/35571

17 JUL 1919

N° 7 a.

Mai 1919.

WAR DIARY
or
INTELLIGENCE SUMMARY.
(Erase heading not required.)

Army Form C. 2118.

Place	Date	Hour	Summary of Events and Information	Remarks and references to Appendices
Wimereux	1/19	—	Q.O.C. inspected the Hospital	
"	7/3/19		A.D.M.S. 38th Div. inspected Hospital	
"	22/3/19		Major Clark demobilized	
"	25/3/19		A.D.M.S. visited hospital + said goodbye on departing	
"	30/3/19		Lieut Col O.M.E. O'Brady handed over command to Capt J. Ross on reporting to 92nd Field Amb	J. Ross Capt R.A.M.C. O.C. 110 F.Amb

WAR DIARY or INTELLIGENCE SUMMARY

Army Form C. 2118.

110th Fd Amb

(Erase heading not required.)

Instructions regarding War Diaries and Intelligence Summaries are contained in F. S. Regs., Part II. and the Staff Manual respectively. Title pages will be prepared in manuscript.

Place	Date	Hour	Summary of Events and Information	Remarks and references to Appendices
Mouveaux	5/4/19		Ambulance open to Cadre Strength	JCPhillips
	7/4/19		Capt. D.V. Burrows returned from leave in U.K.	JCPhillips Capt.
	14/4/19		Capt. D.V. Burrows proceeded to NERVICQ & took over charge of 75th Motor Amb. (Amb A.S.M.S 5" Queen)	JCPhillips Capt.
	22/4/19		Lieut Parnell proceeded on leave U.K. (14 days)	JCPhillips
	28/4/19		Evacuations — Ordinary cases evac to BRUGES COURTRAI SPECIAL cases to 39 STAT. A.S.C.R.	JCR
			Serious during month have been sending men in & stay before to GHENT	
			BRUGES, OSTEND, & ZEEBRUGGE by train routes towards Survey	JCR
				JCBurrow Capt. Name

O.C. 110th Field Amb.
(36th Divn Rest. [ation])

No. 110 Jeddah Arab.

Army Form C. 2118.

110 2nd Aust

WAR DIARY
or
INTELLIGENCE SUMMARY.
(Erase heading not required.)

Place	Date	Hour	Summary of Events and Information	Remarks and references to Appendices
Morbeque	8/5/19		Lt. Cmdr. W. Parnell reported received from leave UK	Ceased US
	18/5/19		Cadre reduced 10 RAMC 4 H.T. ASC demobilized	UR
			Present Cadre (2 Officers) (36 O.R. Name) (4 H.ASC) (3 P.B.)	UR
			Orders received during week that this Unit was to be disbanded.	
			All medical equip. has been handed in to Advanced Medical Stores	
			Whilst awaiting transport to take Ordnance Equip to	UR
			Calais Dn. Nagasanying then Lt. W. Nummy & Rest/Station all patients are evacuated	
			to 62 CCS. Gorbrai	

[Signature]
O.C. 110 Field Amb.

110/3585

110th F.A.

June, 1919

110 3rd Aust Army Form C. 2118.

WAR DIARY
or
INTELLIGENCE SUMMARY.
(Erase heading not required.)

Place	Date	Hour	Summary of Events and Information	Remarks and references to Appendices
6/6/19			Capt T.C Robb RAMC. handed over 110 Field Amb. to Lt QM W.Parvis	WP
7/6/19			All Wagons H.T. handed in to XV Corps. I.C.S. Croix	WP
14/6/19			Ordnance Stores & equipment handed in to E1. I.C.S. Croix.	WP
			Receipts handed over to DADOS 36 Div	WP
17/6/19			All personnel disposed of & unit ceases to exist.	WP

W Parvis Lt QM.
OC 110 Field Amb

17/6/19

www.ingramcontent.com/pod-product-compliance
Lightning Source LLC
Chambersburg PA
CBHW080848230426
43662CB00013B/2052